Scholarly Reprint Series

The Scholarly Reprint Series has been established to bring back into print valuable titles from the University of Toronto Press backlist for which a small but continuing demand is known to exist. Special techniques (including some developed by the University of Toronto Press Printing Department) have made it possible to reissue these works in uniform case bindings in runs as short as 50 copies. The cost is not low, but prices are far below what would have to be charged for such short-run reprints by normal methods.

The Scholarly Reprint Series has proved a valuable help to scholars and librarians, particularly those building new collections. We invite nominations of titles for reissue in this form, and look forward to the day when, with this series and other technological developments, the label 'out of print' will virtually disappear from our backlist.

*Published in association with the
Canadian League of Composers by
University of Toronto Press, 1961*

A report from the International Conference of Composers, held at the Stratford Festival, Stratford, Ontario, Canada, August 1960

The Modern Composer and His World

Edited by John Beckwith & Udo Kasemets with a foreword by Louis Applebaum, Conference Director

COPYRIGHT, CANADA, 1961
UNIVERSITY OF TORONTO PRESS

SCHOLARLY REPRINT SERIES EDITION 1978
REPRINTED IN PAPERBACK 2014

ISBN 978-0-8020-7090-6 (CLOTH)
ISBN 978-1-4426-5177-7 (PAPER)
LC 62-252

FOREWORD

Louis Applebaum

Canada is a very stimulating, satisfying, and happy place in which to live and work. In the arts, especially in music and painting, the present is exciting, the future hopeful. This optimistic, self-satisfied estimate comes out of great personal bias, it is true, but it can be supported by statistics and experience.

As recently as twenty-five years ago, the composer was an uncommon creature in Canada's society, well hidden and rarely audible. The genus could count few members and their total effect on the community was not significant. Whether musicians did or did not create made little basic difference to Canada's musical life, dependent as it was, almost entirely, on the creative exports of the United States, England, and France. We are still large artistic importers, but today our own composers, painters, and writers cannot be ignored. Largely because of the efforts of the pioneer composer-teachers of three decades ago, our music schools can now graduate each year a class of strong-willed, independent, enterprising musical beings. The musical seasons in our cities are now agitated, sometimes violently, by the outpourings of our new creators. Many organizations, like the Canada Council, the Music Centre, the Performing Rights Societies, the Arts Councils, the Festivals, and community groups, are directly involved in what the Canadian composers think and do; and the willing and valuable Canadian Broadcasting Corporation reflects it all. No agency, private or governmental, has striven more anxiously to encourage and develop a national artistic soul and profile, or has achieved more.

Much of Canada's musical individuality can be attributed to the existence and purposeful programming of the CBC.

To the minority of Canadians who concern themselves with the arts, the rather remarkable change in our country has been exciting. On the rest of the world the phenomenon has made little impact. In music, publication is still the principal means of communication, and Canadian works have not been published in any quantity. Though the International Service of the CBC has for years been making recordings of his music available to other countries of the world, the Canadian composer is still a bit of a phantom; in international terms his name has meant little, his music less.

In the fall of 1958 a small group of officials from the Stratford Festival was invited to visit Russia to investigate the prospects for exchanges between the Stratford Festival Company and ensembles from the Soviet Union. As the Festival's Director of Music, I was a member of the group. In Moscow, in the lobby of the Ukrainia Hotel, we were pleasantly surprised to meet Roy Harris, Roger Sessions, Peter Mennin, and Ulysses Kay, the first American composers to present and discuss their music in the Soviet Union. Roy Harris was a former teacher of mine whom I had not seen for many years. The reunion in that setting was so unexpected and meaningful that we both changed our plans for the next day in order to be able to talk. In deference to the setting, I suppose, the conversation dealt mostly with international matters and the significance of the exchanges of views between the American composers and their Russian confrères. With what must have seemed to Mr. Harris foolhardy self-assurance, I offered to try to organize, along lines we discussed in some detail, an international meeting of composers in Canada, preferably in Stratford and, if possible, under the aegis of the Canadian League of Composers.

The League was then a seven-year-old child. As a prodigy it had, through its concert-giving and through its promotion, done much to publicize and expose the music of its members to their countrymen. A project of the size of the proposed conference seemed overly ambitious to even this eager organization. Nothing like it had ever taken place in Canada before. It would cost so much money, take so much effort and time! Would other countries seriously consider it and would the results merit the hard work? The Stratford Festival was interested and willing. Though it would tax facilities and personnel, it seemed to be the kind of project that the Festival should gather under its cloak. The proposed programme of concerts and discussions, the focus of international attention on Stratford, the presence of composers of renown from many countries would enhance Stratford's already enviable reputation.

The Canada Council, the fount of support and encouragement to all that is worth while in the arts, was approached. Though the Council agreed to assist the Conference, it strongly urged, and wisely, the deferment of the project for a year, until the summer of 1960. Now began the lengthy, sometimes frustrating, though usually encouraging correspondence with official musical organizations throughout the world. About thirty-five such societies were contacted in as many countries. Each was asked to select a delegation and to arrange for its arrival in Toronto. From that point on the delegates would be the guests of the Canadian League of Composers during the eight-day period of the Conference.

Then the organizational activities began. A Board of Directors was created to supervise policy. Its members represented the large associations of both Canada and the United States which seemed most directly concerned with the successful outcome of the Conference. In addition to representation from the Canadian League of Composers and the Stratford Festival, the Board included the heads of CAPAC, the Canadian Music Centre, ASCAP, BMI, the American Federation of Musicians, the Los Angeles Music Festival, the CBC, and Roy Harris as director of the International Institute of Music. Monies had to be raised to match the budget; a programme of activities had to be created that would reflect the wide field of interest and satisfy the international character of the meeting; a machinery had to be created to transport, house, and feed our respected guests; the language and translation problem had to be overcome; the interests of our native composers and of our neighbours in the United States had to be considered; the full programme of activities and the complex demands they would make had now to be integrated in detail into the Stratford Festival's operation.

Stratford is a small city of some 20,000 people, nestled in the pleasant farming country of southwest Ontario. Through its centre ambled a little creek which, many years ago, had been converted into an elegant, quiet river, had been renamed Avon, banked by green parks, and sprinkled with peacefully floating canoes, paddle boats, and majestic swans. On a hill overlooking the picnickers who crowd the river's banks, the exuberant baseball players, and the tree-filled park, now stands the magnificent, modern, circular Festival Theatre, lauded as one of the finest theatrical structures in the world. For about five months of the year its unusual platform stage vibrates under the agile leapings and posturings of a company of Shakespearean actors. The Shakespearean Festival, inaugurated in 1953 by culturally ambitious Stratford citizens under the direction and inspiration of Sir Tyrone Guthrie, has each year increased its scope. It now includes an exciting Music Festival, exhibits of paintings, books, and theatrical lore, an International Film Festival, and other auxiliary activities. For about a third of a year this gentle Ontario city becomes the virile cultural centre of the country, a miracle that many Stratfordites still cannot understand, and that many anxious citizens of Toronto (population $1\frac{1}{2}$ million and only 100 miles away) still resent. Into this setting we planned to insert our large-scale International Conference of Composers.

Somehow, it all came to pass. On a sunny Sunday, composers from over twenty countries created a noisy but happy confusion that filled the small office in the Festival Theatre which served as headquarters for the Conference. The greetings, meetings, questionings, and sortings, and the realization that the lengthy and sometimes trying efforts had, at last, brought together the composers we so long anticipated, contributed to a memory we shall long keep intact. Imagine the pleasure in seeing at the opening affair, a banquet that followed the last of the regular Festival concerts (a Beethoven trio programme played by Glenn Gould, Leonard Rose, and Oskar Shumsky), the aggregate of creative musical treasure that had come to Stratford from so many of the world's artistic capitals!

For eight days thereafter, fifty delegates participated in a concentrated programme of panel sessions, concerts, discussions, and diversions. If this Conference can be measured as a success, it would derive, I think, from a few of the principles that were prescribed. We had no wish to either affirm or deny, worship or excommunicate any one creative attitude or technique. We hoped to create an environment in which serial, tonal, electronic, and conventional approaches to composition all could be expounded and defended without embarrassment. There was, at the same time, no geographical bias, no political overtone.

The delegates spent most of every day in each other's company. In addition to attending concerts and entertainments as a group, they also ate all their meals together in Stratford's congenial Country Club. Mealtime gave everyone the chance to relax and to exchange ideas and impressions in a pleasant, informal way. The Stratford Festival turned out to be an ideal setting for this Conference. Opportunities for the delegates to see the Festival Shakespearean productions were carefully integrated into the schedule of activities and served to give to our guests a good impression of the quality of our artistic life. The serenity and beauty of the City of Stratford, which contribute so much to the success of the Festival, served equally on behalf of this Conference.

If our guests from other lands will excuse this selfish comment, the most valuable product of the Conference was the contribution it has made to Canada's musical life. To the Canadian composer it has given a self-respect that is vital and hard to come by. This was achieved simply and effectively by having music by Canadian composers scheduled, criticized, and accepted on the same terms and by the same standards applied to music by the renowned guests. To Canadian audiences the result will be salutary and long-lasting. For the delegates, to most of whom Canadian music had been a mystery, the exposure to our creative activities will bring a reaction that will, at last, be coloured by first-hand experience and knowledge.

Through the efficient and effective actions of the Canadian Broadcasting Corporation, the Conference concerts, as well as interviews and discussions, were carried across Canada. We are very gratified, too, that the International Service of the CBC has received and filled specific requests for Conference material from about sixty different national broadcasting systems. It seems that throughout the world, interest in the Stratford meeting was even more widespread than we expected.

The final purpose of the Conference is reflected in the volume you are now reading. If there is value in making available, in the words of the composers themselves, a collection of opinions on subjects that are of concern to the composer, to the art of musical composition, and to the interested auditor, then these excerpts from the papers and discussions can well serve that end.

LOUIS APPLEBAUM

The Participants in the International Conference of Composers

I

composer-delegates

AUSTRIA	Cesar Bresgen, Karl Schiske
BELGIUM	Victor Legley
CUBA	Aurelio de la Vega
CZECHOSLOVAKIA	Václav Dobiás
DENMARK	Vagn Holmboe
FINLAND	Olavi Pesonen
FRANCE	Henri Dutilleux
GERMANY	Karl Höller, Hermann Reutter
GREAT BRITAIN	Iain Hamilton, Elizabeth Maconchy, Guy Warrack
ISRAEL	Josef Tal
ITALY	Luciano Berio
MEXICO	Ignacio Esperon, Blas Galindo Rodolfo Halffter
NETHERLANDS	Henk Badings
NORWAY	Klaus Egge
POLAND	Zygmunt Mycielski
SWEDEN	Karl-Birger Blomdahl
SWITZERLAND	Constantin Regamey, Heinrich Sutermeister
USA	Hector Campos-Parsi, Roy Harris, Ernst Krenek, Otto Luening, George Rochberg, Gunther Schuller, Vladimir Ussachevsky, Edgard Varèse
USSR	Otar Taktakishvili
CANADA	Murray Adaskin, István Anhalt, Louis Applebaum, Violet Archer, John Beckwith, Claude Champagne, Gabriel Charpentier, Samuel Dolin Marvin Duchow, S. C. Eckhardt-Gramatté,

Robert Fleming, Harry Freedman,
Otto Joachim, Udo Kasemets,
Talivaldis Kenins, Oskar Morawetz,
Jean Papineau-Couture, Kenneth Peacock,
Eldon Rathburn, Harry Somers,
Andrew Twa, John Weinzweig

II

guest observers

CANADA — Jean-Marie Beaudet, executive secretary, Canadian Music Centre; Helmut Blume, McGill University; Franz Kraemer, Canadian Broadcasting Corporation; W. St. Clair Low, general manager, Composers Authors and Publishers Association of Canada; Sir Ernest MacMillan; Geoffrey Waddington, director of music, Canadian Broadcasting Corporation

USA — Oliver Daniel, Broadcast Music Inc.; Alfred V. Frankenstein, critic, *San Francisco Chronicle;* Mrs. Jean Reti; Howard Shanet, conductor; Leon Stein; Anton Wolf

OTHER COUNTRIES — Guillermo Espinosa, director, Inter-American Music Center, Pan-American Union; Vassily Kukharski, USSR, critic; Jan Matějček, Czechoslovakia, critic

III

sponsoring organizations

Canadian League of Composers
Stratford Shakespearean Festival Foundation of Canada
Canada Council
Canadian Broadcasting Corporation
Composers Authors and Publishers Association of Canada
BMI Canada Limited
Broadcast Music Inc.
American Society of Composers Authors and Publishers
American Federation of Musicians of the United States and Canada
International Music Council (UNESCO)

CONTENTS

Foreword by Louis Applebaum v

The Participants in the International Conference of Composers x

I The Composer in Today's World

COMPOSER AND PUBLIC
Victor Legley (BELGIUM). Vassily Kukharski (USSR). Alfred Frankenstein (USA): *The Critic's Role. Discussion.* **3**

TRAINING OF COMPOSERS
Heinrich Sutermeister (SWITZERLAND): *Letter to a Young Aspiring Composer.* Jean Papineau-Couture (CANADA). Aurelio de la Vega (CUBA). *Discussion.* **17**

COMPOSER AND PERFORMER
Václav Dobiás (CZECHOSLOVAKIA). Gunther Schuller (USA). Victor Feldbrill (CANADA). *Discussion.* **35**

II The Composer's Métier

SERIALISM
Iain Hamilton (GREAT BRITAIN). George Rochberg (USA): *Duration in Music.* Ernst Krenek (USA). *Discussion.* **49**

SOME OTHER PATHS
Henri Dutilleux (FRANCE): *Diversities in Contemporary French Music.* Zygmunt Mycielski (POLAND). Constantin Regamey (SWITZERLAND). Gunther Schuller (USA). **77**

OPERA AND BALLET
Karl-Birger Blomdahl (SWEDEN): *Aniara.* Henk Badings (NETHERLANDS): *Experiences with Electronic Ballet Music.* **102**

SYNTHETIC MEANS
Hugh LeCaine (CANADA). Josef Tal (ISRAEL). Vladimir Ussachevsky (USA). *Discussion.* **109**

FORM
Vagn Holmboe (DENMARK): *On Form and Metamorphosis.* Luciano Berio (ITALY). *Discussion.* **134**

III Summary

Conference Summary by Marvin Duchow. *Discussion.* **151**

The Concerts of the Conference by Udo Kasemets **163**

Editors' Note

This volume has not been envisioned as a transcript of the International Conference of Composers. Therefore, some omissions, abbreviations, and rearrangements of material, including some individual papers and discussions, seemed in order. Our aim has been to produce an accurate, and at the same time a clearly focussed, account of this unusually varied and free-wheeling week of talk.

The Conference languages were English, French, German, Russian, and Czech. Simultaneous short-wave translations were made in the hall for the first three. For purposes of this book, the French and German papers have been freshly translated. For the Czech and Russian papers, the Conference translator's versions were used. In addition, some French-language portions of the Conference discussions have been newly translated by the editors.

We acknowledge the generous assistance of the Canadian Broadcasting Corporation in making available tape recordings of all panel sessions of the Conference. We have especially valued the patient help and interest of Carl Little, CBC music producer, Toronto; John Roberts, CBC national music department, Toronto; and Percy Tollman, CBC International Service, Montreal.

J.B.
U.K.

Part One
The Composer in Today's World

COMPOSER AND PUBLIC

Victor Legley (BELGIUM)

One might begin a discussion of this vexed question by stating, rather bluntly, that over the last fifty years the public has almost become a factor which does not count. For some years the only active part left for them to play in musical life has been strictly limited to the payment of an entrance fee. For the rest, the composer seems to have decided once and for all that the public didn't understand him or his work. The public very soon reacted in the easiest way: they deserted the concert halls. I fear my country is not the only one where one modern work on a programme is sufficient to make the public decide to go to a football match instead. In very recent years, not only the organizers, but also the composers, have, however, discovered that it is necessary to bridge the abyss between themselves and the public.

When looking upon the dreary reality that this or that musical work is not understood by the public, we often hear the composer put forward certain claims, for instance, that the music of a Wagner was not understood either, when performed for the first time. Indeed it does take a certain time for the public to get acquainted with new sounds. But we should not forget that these same works met with enormous success a short time after their first performances. Quite different are the present circumstances, when some music—of which I will be the first to recognize the great value—is still not understood thirty and more years after being written, and when we know that in the meantime the possibilities of having it performed have increased enormously.

The organizers always try to find a way of interesting their public by explaining, by commenting on music before the performances. I am sorry, but I don't believe very much in this. I always have the impression that people never listen to explanations. (I don't either.) They only wait politely till the explanations are over, to get what they came for: the music itself. The more interested members of the public, who genuinely wish to know more, can very easily find a great deal to read about whatever it is they wish to know. . . . There are composers who spend more of their time explaining their music than writing it. I can't help feeling there must be something wrong with music that needs so much explanation.

The worst of all ways of explaining music is by giving a technical analysis of it. It only bores the public. People are not interested in knowing if a work is serial, and if the series is standing on its head or lying on its side. It can be awfully interesting for the technicians themselves, but the public is only interested in the audible results; and if these are not sufficient to keep their attention, neither comments nor explanations will make them change their mind.

The speaker noted the way in which radio and recordings, by making music more readily available, have influenced concert life by inducing casual ways of listening to works of music. He also observed that radio and recordings have lessened the music-lover's desire to make music himself.

One of the first things to be done in order to form a new concert public is to teach people again the pleasure of playing music, to make the interest in amateurism grow once again. Isn't it evident that it is precisely chamber music that has lost the greatest part of its public?

Musical competitions, such as the contests for the Queen Elizabeth of Belgium Prize, were mentioned as successful ventures, appealing, however, to a public more interested in competition than in music. Their destructive effect on entrants, through the narrowing of both their repertoire and the aims of their professional preparation, was also cited.

So in the end everyone seems to be guilty, in this very complex question of composer and public. It would take us a long time to study to what degree the composers themselves are guilty. The public has certainly lost its way in this gigantic chaos of modern music. They can no longer follow the various ways that various composers claim as the only true ones for the future of music. Composers who wish to continue writing in a more traditional way are regularly treated as old-fashioned by the ultra-modernists, who, in their turn, are treated as mere makers of strange noises by the former. Both are wrong. The public concludes that composers are a very strange kind of creature and lose their interest.

We could paraphrase a great French statesman and say that music is too important a thing to be left only in the hands of musicians. . . . Whether we like it or not, we should not forget that people will never be interested in going to a concert to solve problems. There are too many problems in music nowadays. There are too many composers more interested in the problem than in the result. People don't worry about problems. If they don't find music, they stay at home. And—whether we like it or not—in the end it is always the public that is going to be right.

Vassily Kukharski (U.S.S.R.)

This theme (composer and public) has been considered contemporary at all times in the history of music, beginning with the time of Bach. For every really creative composer, the public has been considered a partner co-operating in the production of his work, and at the same time a judge, an arbiter of his work—or, in other words, a court of highest reference in judging the value of his production. But relations between the composer and his public have assumed an ever-increasing acuity with time. As one German music critic put it recently, there are two types of music—one type is played and the other type is criticized in newspapers! But *both* these types of music are called modern music.

What is modern music?

For our predecessors, modern music and progressive music were synonymous terms. Every real art is inextricably linked with the concept of man; every true art is created by men for men in full harmony with the spirit of the times. For we want to see the activity of every modern artist directed towards the people. We want the modern musician to consider his work not as a hobby, nor as a means of expressing his own inventions or fictions. Every production of a composer becomes, by the very fact that he has produced it, not only his own work, but the work of his people and the work of his epoch. And just as the painter must observe the existing world, so the composer must listen to the existing sounds.

The modern composer must understand modern man. He must understand and appreciate his ardour, the faith of man today in the virtues of reason. Music should avoid making men lazy or indifferent; music should avoid the dangers of making or encouraging listeners to become impoverished in their thoughts; music should avoid the dangers of productions that would simply express the spirit of "each man for himself." Only music that does avoid these dangers can truly be called modern music. Only such types of music can truly deserve the designation of "progressive."

Unfortunately progress has now been designated in another fashion. This other interpretation of art arose at the beginning of the twentieth century, with the thesis of art for art's sake—and it rapidly deteriorated into the thesis of art for the sake of a chosen few. Progress was defined as the production of new unprecedented forms, and everything traditional was considered obsolete. But this in substance was simply a pretext invented by those who really had nothing to say, who simply tried to invent new works and new terms to conceal the sterility of their own talent. This was simply artificial "progress," because these artists overlooked the real, the vital element in their work—that is, the element of man.

These radical trends in music have created a new type of musical amateur. He might be called the philistine of music. Previously philistines were designated as those who accepted only traditional forms and who denied the validity of all new productions. But could we not call that person, or that critic of art, who approves and who extols the praises of anything new merely because it is new, could we not with greater reason designate *this* person as a philistine? And thus we can place in a similar category many of the new phenomena such as *musique concrète*, and so on.

Periodically, panic arises amongst composers. When the wheel was invented, the musicians at that time also began to raise certain questions: "Isn't it time to throttle the song of the nightingale and to muffle it with the sounds of a creaking wagon-wheel? " Listening to the sounds of these creaking wheels, these would-be musicians seized any kind of drum or percussion instrument, and tried to imitate the creaking. Today history is repeating itself. As one of the protagonists of the school of dodecaphonism said: "The bomb is exploding unharmoniously!"

We passed through this trend in our country during the 1920's and 1930's. In western Europe and in America, perhaps you were not very well informed about the representatives of these trends in our country, but at that time such composers as Schoenberg, Alban Berg, and Krenek began to be played very frequently, and thereafter the Russian modern composers followed this trend. But this fashion was not very long-lived and here the public—the great counsellor and friend—had its word to say. The public rose to its feet against such productions. This same thing occurred in France, Austria, and in many other countries, and, as I read in one French newspaper, there arose at that time a divorce between the public and the so-called new music.

It may not be true that a single voice in the crowd may be wrong, but in any case the whole public has expressed its own taste. Naturally, for some it is possible for a certain time to influence and to intimidate the public, but you cannot for very long make the public consider something worthless as beautiful and worthwhile. The composer must therefore remain on his guard.

The composer and artist not only learns from the public, but his task is also to teach the public and to inculcate the tenets of good taste. The composer must always listen attentively to, but must not be subservient to his public. He must, through his contact with the public, create works which will have sense and meaning for them, and by so doing reach their very heart.

This is the true *avant-garde* of our modern art today. The greatest representatives of this true modern art are Honegger, Georges Auric, Prokofiev, Sibelius, Janacek, Shostakovitch, Kodály, Britten, Khatchaturian, Villa-Lobos, Václav Dobiás, Ralph Vaughan Williams, Bartók, Orff. The true music of today unites amongst its ranks all those who are attentive to the aspirations of our times and to the ideals and feelings of men in the world today. The true music of today has acquired a very broad public. The productions of a great group of American composers have come much closer to this great public. Here I am thinking of Barber, Copland, Menotti, Macdowell, and Roy Harris. The present and the future are in favour of such music.

M. Drouin's speech of yesterday[1] can be summarized as a message or an appeal for co-operation through friendly relations among

[1]The Hon. Mark Drouin, Speaker of the Senate, Ottawa, had addressed the opening banquet of the Composers' Conference.

composers for the purpose of bringing countries closer together. His words were filled with expectation and hope for a great flourishing in the cultural life of Canada. Excuse me for being frank, but I take the liberty of saying the following: The great task of Canadian musicians and composers today lies not in the comparison of the relative merits of electronic music and *musique concrète* with other new musical avenues, but rather in the creation of a dynamic, creative Canadian music, music which will be filled and permeated with the very life-blood and spirit of the Canadian people. This is a very difficult task. Of course it would be easier to study the mathematical systems of these new music forms. But this, in my eyes, is the true and the main goal to be achieved. You must find your own road. You must pave this road through unexplored regions.

As Dmitri Shostakovitch has said: "Both the present and the future belong to really genuine music, and the present and the future are directed towards great artistic productions, in the inspiration of a high humanism—an art which would unite people, and which would be directed at the great masses of people, and not at a very narrow clique of specialists; an art which would inculcate in people noble and high ideals and a high ethical sense."

Alfred Frankenstein (USA). *The Critic's Role*

The history of musical composition is examined in a new survey at least once a week, and big tomes are likewise devoted to the history of musical performance, but the history of musical criticism has been written only once, at least in the English language. The author of that history was Dr. Max Graf, who had for many years been music critic of the *Neue Freie Presse* in Vienna. Strangely enough, Dr. Graf never asks the crucial question, "Why musical criticism?", but in the course of his book he nevertheless provides the answer, if without much realization of the fact that he has done so.

Dr. Graf points out, as one of the odd, unmeaningful aspects of his story, the fact that musical criticism began to appear in European newspapers at the moment when Johann Sebastian Bach and other creative souls of the mid-eighteenth century began to part company with their hearers. When the Leipzig audience of the

1740's found itself unable to follow where Bach was leading, when bewilderment at the hare-brained experimentalism of the modernists started to reach alarming proportions, just at that moment, says Graf, journalistic musical criticism made its appearance on the world scene. Dr. Graf sees no special significance in this, but it is obviously a fact of the very highest significance. It provides musical criticism with a rationale and a reason for being. Nothing else does.

Whether we like it or not—and many dislike it intensely—there has been a gap between composer and audience for the past three hundred years. It is the function of musical criticism to close that gap, so far as a structure of words can do so; perhaps it would be better to say that it is the function of musical criticism to speed the closure rather than effect it, for criticism, obviously, cannot take the place of art, and, Mr. E. M. Forster to the contrary notwithstanding, no critic pretends it does.

If this be so, it follows that the critic must be endlessly curious about the new music of his time, must constantly be exploring the new ideas and adventuring along the new frontiers of the art he has chosen to serve. If he is unable to do this, he should not be a music critic; and in all probability, music critics, like dancers and baseball players, should be retired early. As a matter of fact, most of us retire ourselves without knowing it, for we gradually slip from being critics of music to being critics of musicians, which is a profoundly different thing. I should be the last person on earth to deny that the performance of music is a great and subtle art, but when a critic finds himself more interested in performers than composers, when he finds himself preferring Beethoven and Brahms under a famous baton to the new chamber music offered on the same evening by the local Composers' Forum, he has ceased to uphold the only standard which justifies the existence of his profession.

But, you say, the criticism of new music is always wrong, and you adduce famous historical examples to prove it. On this head, several things of importance are to be said.

Not long ago Nicolas Slonimsky published a *Lexicon of Musical Invective*, tracing critical obtuseness through the centuries. The book is full of things like this: "What, then, is music nowadays—harmony, melody, content, form—when this rigmarole seriously pretends to be regarded as music? If the composer intends to mystify his followers with this newest work, if he wants to make fun of their brainless veneration, then, of course, the case is different, and we salute in him the greatest faker of this century and of all future millennia."

In these few lines the critic has employed two or three of the classic formulae of musical incomprehension, asserting that the work under discussion is evidence of the decline of music in the critic's own time, that those who like it obviously have something the matter with them, and that the composer is a fraud. Just such statements are made over and over and over again by the least informed, the least intelligent, and the most thoroughly incompetent; usually we dismiss them as the ravings of the ignorant and as evidence of the fact that criticism invariably fails to perceive the virtues of new works. But what shall we say when, as in this instance, the composer is Brahms and the critic is Hugo Wolf? Similarly, it was not a professional critic, but Karl Maria von Weber, who declared after the first performance of Beethoven's seventh symphony that its composer should be confined in a madhouse; and the very first specimen in Slonimsky's *Lexicon of Invective*—the observation that the music of Béla Bartók is "mere ordure"—was likewise the work of a respected if not a celebrated composer, Frederick Corder.

My point is this: although artists often insist that no one has the right to assume a critical stance unless he has had experience in the art criticized, the record shows that composers themselves have been no less silly in their reactions to the new music of other composers than have the rest of us. A trained ear and a profound knowledge of compositional techniques, in other words, do not prevent narrowness or incomprehension and do not provide their possessors with a licence to serve as critics. Criticism, like composition itself, requires a knack or gift of its own; training enhances it, but, in criticism as in everything else, technique is no substitute for talent.

Criticism, in this sense, is an independent art, and I use the word "art" advisedly. Criticism is not—most distinctly not—a science, although numerous efforts to place it on a scientific basis have been made, from the mathematical tables of evaluation which were so characteristic of the eighteenth century to the semantic and psychological analyses which are so characteristic of our own time. All these attempts to create a science of criticism have failed, but in today's view the most absurd are those which have sought or pretended to establish objective rules for value judgment in any of the arts.

In the late eighteenth century Dr. Charles Burney analysed certain madrigals by Carlo Gesualdo in order to show that this composer was a mere dilettante and something of a fraud. A hundred and fifty years later the English musicologist, Scott Goddard, analysed very much the same music in very much the same terms in order to show that Gesualdo was one of the most profoundly original geniuses of all time. The analysis was the same, the conclusions diametrically opposed. From this—and the case is far from unique—one may conclude that the real basis of the value judgment lay, with both critics, not in the facts brought forth by the analysis but in deep, unconscious layers of personality determined by individual experience.

Contemporary criticism, because it realizes these things, makes much less show of value judgment than criticism formerly did. Today we are unlikely to make a clear-cut stand on a question of value, saying that this or that work is good or bad; today we are likely to disguise our evaluation as description, telling what the work was like, but nonetheless conveying our reactions to it. Our descriptions, furthermore, are far less "literary" than those of an older generation. The prose poem is out, and even the purple patch. Styles in criticism, in other words, mirror styles in the arts criticized. When I was young, criticism was in its impressionistic stage. Today it is in its neo-classical phase; eventually, you may rest assured, it will reflect serialism, electronicism, and Webernian pointillism as well, not so much in what it says as in something far more important—the way it says it.

Criticism, in other words, is a mirror of the arts and not their foe. To be sure, there is no critic without his limitations, and a critic who delighted in everything equally would be a pretty poor specimen of his breed. Still and all, breadth of view is essential, and herein lies one of the major differences between the critic and the artist. The composer must believe passionately in his idiom and the performer must believe with the utmost fervour in his method of interpretation; it is these convictions that make for quality in the composer and the performer, but the very intensity of belief necessary for the composer or executant is likely to work against him when he assumes the role of critic.

In facing the world of contemporary music the critic must, as we have seen, be enormously interested, full of curiosity, and eager to know what is going on. At the same time, he is likely to develop a kind of tolerant skepticism toward his art as a whole. In the English-speaking countries of North America there are perhaps 10,000 composers of serious music now at work. Of these, less than one per cent are well known and, in all probability, at least 75 per cent are destined never to have any kind of hearing at all. And yet the 9,900 have their role in history, for there is a law in human affairs as in biology which necessitates the proliferation of thousands of organisms in order that one may survive.

The critic in the concert hall has to make a stab at estimating if the new work he is hearing is one of the crowd or one of the masterpieces for which the crowd exists. He may often be wrong. Perhaps he will be wrong more often than right. But if his value judgments are more often with than against the modern composer, he is likely to be right a good bit of the time.

Discussion

John Beckwith (CANADA): No one has defined what the public is. Possibly in this discussion one should not talk of the public, but of the publics, plural, because we have a situation today where the composers are not faced with a single defined public, but a large undefined public made up of a lot of minorities.

I noticed the remark of Mr Legley, "In the end it is always the public that is going to be right." Or, as Mr Kukharski put it, the public is the "supreme court." I wonder if there is general agreement on that, or if sometimes the panel members feel, as I feel myself, that the public is very fickle, and from generation to generation changes its point of view.

Mr Legley, in reply, referred to Wolf's opinions of Brahms, cited in Mr Frankenstein's paper. "Yet, in the long run, Brahms was accepted."

Beckwith: Yes, Brahms gained popularity—but over a period of fifty years, and only in some countries.

Legley: Success varies always from country to country. Take the case of Mahler.

Beckwith: You were speaking of the pianists' competition of Queen Elizabeth of Belgium, and you mentioned the restricted repertoire of most of the contestants. Is it not true that the finalists in the contest are required to prepare on very short notice a specially composed new concerto? How does this work? Is it successful?

Legley: Yes; there is always a modern work written especially for the contest. There are twelve finalists. The work is played twelve times during the contest. Afterwards nowhere, never again, does one hear it played.

Beckwith: Does that situation continue then, or has it been abandoned?

Legley: I believe it will continue.

Helmut Blume (CANADA, *chairman*): I believe in order to clarify this relation with the public now, and the public in the future, one should also keep in mind that there is a certain margin by which the public will become the accepting or the refusing public. For instance, take a case like *Rite of Spring* by Stravinsky, which actually caused combat in the concert hall when it was first performed; it has now become a perfectly acceptable piece.

Our other panelist, Mr Pesonen, has remarked that a piece must have something to say. Something to say to whom? If it says something to me, does it mean that the piece is good? Is it good only for me? In other words, we are really discussing the possibility of absolutes in evaluation of art. I'll never forget one remark of Hindemith: "Suppose a student comes to me and shows me a new symphony and I look at it and I say, 'Well, here the technique is not very good and here the craft could be better, and on the whole I don't like it.' Then the student will say to me, 'That's too bad—but *I* like it!'" So, Hindemith said, "I've got to have more to give him than simply a criticism of his technique, or the expression of my personal taste." But it seems we are no closer to reaching these absolute standards yet.

Leon Stein (USA): The big problem, I think, is to distinguish between the reputably correct and the aesthetically true. In all circumstances these two have been at variance: sometimes it's a clique; and perhaps in Russia it might be a kind of state pressure, as to what the reputably correct might be, rather than the aesthetically true. I think, in the long run, it becomes a matter for the critic and perhaps for the public, of anticipating what the ultimate trend is going to be.

Olavi Pesonen (FINLAND): Mr Frankenstein said the public doesn't like the new music, in whatever idiom. That I doubt, because the public likes, for instance, new dance music and light music very much indeed.

Frankenstein: I believe I was slightly misunderstood. I am profoundly convinced that there are elements of these many publics (and I would agree that there is this division of the public into numerous kinds of public) that do accept new idioms and do accept new works. My point was simply that that element of the public which does dislike new idioms is likely to dislike anything new whether it is in a new idiom or an old one.

One more thing, on this question of the public and the publics. Let me use another historical analogy. For about a hundred years after the death of Johann Sebastian Bach, his music was almost totally unknown. Little of it was published. Burney expressed himself of the opinion that old Johann Sebastian was a marvellous organist, but that the real composers of the Bach family were the sons. The public had decided that Bach didn't amount to much. How long does the public verdict last? One wonders if the ultimate acceptance of Bach does not suggest the possibility that the small esoteric minority sometimes—not always, but once in a while—is right.

Now, the re-discovery for the public of Bach's music was the result of an act of great courage on the part of a person who was both performer and composer, namely Mendelssohn, when he dared to perform the *St. Matthew Passion* around 1830 in Leipzig. Perhaps the most profoundly critical of all critical acts is not the act of anyone in my profession at all, but the act of the performer. The most essential critics are the people who decide what we are going to hear. If we are going to perform composition X we are not going to perform composition Y, and this is an act of criticism, compared to which a lifetime spent in writing for newspapers is of no importance whatsoever.

Kukharski: The example you have given of Bach, is, of course, a very advantageous one. The listeners to Bach's music were at the beginning limited to a very small group. But how can we compare the means at our disposal today for propagandizing music, and circulating it, with the means that were available at the time of Bach? Today there are a great many means to hear music at the disposal of the public, and the public chooses what it wishes to listen to—and it makes a very correct choice, in my opinion.

Blume: What is the rate of the works of modern composers actually being performed in Russia on the radio and television and in the concert hall for the Russian public to be able to make a choice?

Kukharski: In my first statement I gave a listing of those modern composers who are very widely played in the Soviet Union today. Allow me to make a second observation in answer to the question, "Who is at fault, the composer or the public?" I believe that it is the composer who is at fault in the eyes of the public, rather than the public who is guilty in the eyes of the composer. The composer comes before the public, as in a play the playwright comes before the public, to be judged—and not the public before the playwright. It is the task of the composer and the musicologist to educate the public; and we begin this educative process in the secondary schools, where we begin the training of the future music listeners. The composer therefore must not only be a creator, but he should also be a propagandist of musical knowledge.

It was stated that perhaps in the Soviet Union it is the state that defines or determines "taste"—what is good in musical productions. If you consider such personalities as Shostakovitch, Kabalevsky, Khatchaturian, Taktakishvili—if you consider these artists as "the state," then you may say it is indeed the state which defines taste. Questions of music are decided and defined by the musicians.

An observer (USA): Is it not so much technical, material criteria which decide the distinction between, let us say, good and bad music, but rather idealistic ones? The question I would like to put to Mr Kukharski is: does he deny *a priori* that modern music—whether it be called pointillistic, dodecaphonic, and so on—is able to be good music? The distinction is not a material one; it's not the technique which *a priori* excludes the music from having a humanitarian character or being useful for the people. I ask Mr Kukharski, can we logically claim that new techniques—let's say those of the twelve-tone system—are unable to produce good music?

To be more precise, we heard the names Scriabin and Bartók and Hindemith. Names do not say very much—only the works. I would be glad to know if the last sonatas of Scriabin, and *Prometheus* are performed in Russia; and what kind of Bartók do they like to hear?

Kukharski: I described the criteria utilized in my country as well as I was able. I enumerated a list of composers who are all known to you, and you know that these composers are not similar to each other, that they differ amongst themselves. The position of the public was not determined by any *a priori* judgment, but rather on the basis of practical experience, in interpretations before the public.

I think that there was expressed a certain slightly naïve fear that Scriabin would not be played in the Soviet Union. But after all, Scriabin is a classical Russian composer. The Tenth Sonata is played very often; Richter is very fond of the last sonatas of Scriabin; and generally all the sonatas of Scriabin are played in the Soviet Union. Bartók is also played very widely: there was a recent musical competition in the Moscow Conservatory on the best interpretation of Bartók.

The difficulty is that we still don't know each other well enough, and many obsolete conceptions are still in vogue in our ideas about each other. If you look at the subject in all calmness, and objectively, you will see that the differences between us are not so great.

TRAINING OF COMPOSERS

Heinrich Sutermeister (SWITZERLAND). *Letter to a Young Aspiring Composer*

You write that you would like to prove to your friends and, last but not least, to yourself that you have something worthwhile to be expressed. Thus your next attempt will be to pay a personal visit to a good publishing house. (The experience that a modern giant publishing company returns the submitted scores without examining them, you will have already behind you.) You take your most recent score and meet a lector who explains politely, yet resolutely, that in 999 cases contemporary music is bad business. The publishing houses have only limited resources at their disposal; nevertheless, a world première in prominent circumstances would be of some assistance.

So far, so good. You take heart and present yourself to a conductor. If you are lucky and he can find a spare minute on his way from the podium to the artists' room or while reading the wires concerning his next engagements, he will throw a quick glance on the opening and closing bars of your score and ask then the ominous question: "When will this work be published?" You see, then, the gruesome *circulus vitiosus* is already closing itself.

Once more you gain courage and knock at the door of an established composer. There too you meet nervous restlessness. The phone rings, the luggage is unpacked, and the next music festival is already near at hand. I shall still rest for a while on the assumption that the successful colleague will have understanding for your problems which, once upon a time, were also his. A short conversation will then show you completely new, unexpected aspects. Every creative activity has to be preceded by a conscious determination of an objective. The first opus to reach the public has to bear the seal of the caste of your ideology. Only then is your appearance legitimate. What you have to say in the spirit of one or another group is decisive. His advice is: "Be discovered! Yet make up your mind by whom you wish to be discovered—this may decisively influence your future career."

Now I shall ask you the important question: What will you do? Will you possess enough inner strength, enough faith in your individuality to withstand the temptations I have suggested? Do not underestimate the urge, so fitting at your age, of exchanging the isolation of an artist for a tie with a group idea.

If you follow the advice of your mentor, you will sacrifice your own artistic responsibilities for the aims of the group which you desire to join. The rules of a tonal system or a metric scheme turn into by-laws of ideology, and you will believe that you have found the firm foundations for which you have been searching in vain. You will soon become as intolerant as your adviser towards other artistic streams, and thus you will join the unhealthy fight for power that dominates the musical life of our day.

But believe me: in this way you will make a career for yourself. The means by which you defend your musical position become extreme; the critics pay you attention, the alert publisher will call, and the first commissions will come in. Soon you will find yourself in the same enviable position as your former adviser. You will have students, and you will give them hints, similar to those you once received.

Yet one day, you will face the unhappy cognizance that you are no longer at the top of the ghostly cavalcade. New names, who in their turn widen and dissect the tonal materials, perk up at your right and left. The number of commissions drops, the publisher writes his first refusal, and the critics are silent. Burnt out and resigned, you try to find a position in the line and drop into anonymity.

My dear friend, with this ruthless parable I want to show you how completely new, how dangerous the situation of our day really is. It demands from each work of art a new independence. Symbols which accompanied the generations before us are emptied of their meaning and it does not matter if we write serial, pointillistic, electronic, neo-baroque or neo-classical music. There is no escape, not even by the way of a cleverly constructed system such as twelve-tone technique, from the overpowering classical or romantic repertoire or the choking, vital superiority of Wagnerian affectation. We are untalented children of ingenious ancestors and we carry a burden of heritage which filled even a man of Arthur Honegger's stature with bitterness towards the musical past. You will reply that it is our right and duty to give a musical interpretation of our time. But why do the concert halls remain empty when a modern work is announced? The average listener has become very suspicious and senses behind the cabalistic codification of the present-day musical language the flatness and emptiness of a faithless time.

With justification, you will be expecting now my own stand on these matters. I found in the *Wiener Musikzeitung* from the year 1827 the following philistine sentences: "One cannot feel well since the 'thinking' composer has neglected grace and beauty for sheer reflection, for painful struggle towards truth. Even if any of these modern art-tormentors ever succeeds in apprehending and moving his listeners through employing his fearsome art-machinery, it will be a miserably torturing, heart-pressing, chokingly horrifying rather than a true, enjoyable, soothing, heart-expanding experience —a far cry from the soul-lifting, exulting artistic pleasures that can be evoked only by the unartificial effusion of a genius."

All these attempts (for instance, the tones created by electronic means), these dissolutions of our tone-world into the smallest particles, remind me of the little boy who spanks the table with which he has collided. Affected negation, indeed open hate, have taken the place of a more fruitful exploration of the ideas of our spiritual ancestors and models. It is not new music that one wants; the desire is for new material, for a new box of toy bricks, with the hope that, thus, one can create a new spirit. Is there not here a lesson to be learned from the nineteenth century, a century that some would like to erase from the history of music, but also a century that brought forth Verdi, who in his later works showed a way from material to man? Thus the lyricism of Desdemona in the last act of *Otello* appears to me more as a beginning than an end. And does not the instrumentation of *Falstaff* constitute a final victory over the weightiness of material? The voices float freely in space and secret forces behind singing humans are the sole determinants of musical happenings.

The way we decide to employ the world of tones to express our present experiences remains a personal matter. Nevertheless, the warmth and transparency of the human image has to prevail. We composers are in the possession of an immense power which we have inherited, which we have learned to manage, and which we will hand over to the coming generations. Let us be aware of this responsibility, and let us try to loosen the grip of short-sighted cliques and the power groups that rule the present music world in an unhealthy manner.

[*translated from the German by* UDO KASEMETS]

Jean Papineau-Couture (CANADA)

From time immemorial the training of composers has been highly controverted.

By applying the same criterion to all creative artists as to poets, the Latin saying *Nascuntur poetae, fiunt oratores* has frequently been used by those who claim that a composer does not need to learn but can rely solely on his natural gifts. Of course, no serious musician has ever entertained such theories, but the question nevertheless arises as to exactly what the composer-to-be should learn under present-day conditions.

Nearly all composers and composition teachers admit that the traditional tonal system, even in its most advanced developments, is nowadays all but obsolete. Does it not therefore follow that the academic study of harmony, counterpoint, and fugue should be discarded? On the other hand, no other system presents such a universal character that it can replace the old standard system. In spite of the very widespread use of the terms "dodecaphony" and "serialism," they are used with such different meanings by various persons that there could hardly be found a better illustration of the Latin saying, *tot capita, quot sensus*. And I do not mean here minor differences in the interpretation of details or a tendency to give greater prominence to one aspect rather than to another, but basic differences pertaining to the construction of the series and to its subsequent manipulations, and even to the meaning and essence of the twelve-tone system and to the elements that can or must undergo a serial treatment. By the multiplicity of its interpretations, the serial dodecaphonic system is eminently unsuitable to form the *basis* of the training of the young composer, but naturally he must be familiar with it.

It is incumbent on the master to inculcate in his pupil knowledge of two different orders: on the one hand, technique, which is the ability to juggle all the musical elements so as to have immediately at hand a maximum number of solutions for any problem in composition, and, on the other hand, aesthetics, a state of mind toward composition itself, imponderable, yet dominating technique.

Let us first deal with the more easily defined element, technique, and revert to the question already stated: Are the traditional studies of harmony, counterpoint, and fugue still necessary nowadays? I unhesitatingly reply in the affirmative; but such studies must be pursued in a very different spirit from that of, let us say, thirty or forty years ago. As long as the tonal system was regarded as law, these traditional studies taught each element of the musical language by a process of more or less exact assimilation of its historical evolution.

At the present time these subjects should be viewed in the same light as Latin and Greek in Graeco-Latin humanities.

Just as one does not study Greek or Latin so as to be able to speak or write it, but as a means of analysis, an *in vitro* experiment for breaking down and reconstructing a verbal mechanism, a rhetorical effect, or even a poetic structure, in the same way, the tonal means, clarified by traditional writing-exercises, provide the budding composer with a safe neutral medium uninfluenced by factors of personal taste, enabling him to manoeuvre amidst the innumerable possible sound combinations.

But in order that the student may derive the maximum benefit from such studies, they must clearly bring out the difference between rules which have an acoustical or physiological justification or basis, rules which are the result of the style of a particular period or of some historical situation, and finally, rules which have been imagined merely to limit the field of exploration of the novice or, on the contrary, to develop the skill of the beginner by multiplying the obstacles so as to compel him to find new solutions.

All this should be complemented by a serious study of musical acoustics, centred more particularly on the physiology of audition, on the one hand, and on the vibrational phenomena as produced by the various instruments and modified by the transmitting medium, on the other. For there is no escaping the fact that a thorough knowledge of musical acoustics is the only immutable basic foundation on which the composer can rely. Whether he is giving his pupil a purely scholastic training or is guiding him in the elaboration of his own personal style, the teacher must always refer back judiciously to the acoustic fundamentals. Anyone hoping to make a success of teaching composition must therefore have a thorough knowledge of this science. And, to state things plainly, a knowledge of acoustics is not rife among musicians. There is in this respect a serious gap that should be filled, and I wish to emphasize that, notwithstanding all the controversies on the subject, physiological acoustics is at the present time the sole value that does not vary according to individual tastes or with the present-day mania for novelty which is rampant in certain quarters.

It is therefore when they are buttressed by a sound knowledge of acoustics that the various traditional or new techniques absorbed by the composer-to-be will acquire their full value. The study of this science should be begun as early as possible, that is, as soon as the student's basic education has fitted him to assimilate its strictly scientific aspect.

(Here I wish to make a distinction: by musical acoustics I do not mean that learning which is indispensable to whoever writes *musique concrète* or electronic music; such knowledge, though involving some acoustics, actually falls under the heading of electronics and may very well be left to those who intend to venture into this very broad but highly specialized musical field. Their numbers are doubtless increasing, but they are still very far from including all composers.)

Having thus acquired a sufficiently clear knowledge of physiological acoustics, the young composer will be in a much better position to acquire proficiency in the various contemporary techniques: polytonality and atonality, dodecaphony and serialism, quarter-tones and exotic scales, and so on, while at the same time realizing the transcendental musical values which are, after all, the true rationale of this art and which are served by each of the different techniques used in turn.

The young composer will thus be provided with an objective criterion by which he can himself judge his writings, and it is only when he is equipped with this indispensable tool that he can truly benefit from a systematic exploration of all the various present-day techniques.

Among all these techniques, the twelve-tone is, by its rational organization, undoubtedly the most enriching for the student, provided, of course, it is not presented, as is all too often the case, as a sort of panacea to confer excellence on the most insignificant musical idea and to convert trash into a masterpiece!

I am taking the liberty of pointing out that, at the Faculty of Music of the University of Montreal, for the past seven years all students have been required to follow a course of lectures on physiological acoustics before undertaking the study of composition proper. Moreover, as both these subjects are taught by the same professor, it is all the easier for him to establish the necessary parallels, comparisons, and interrelations between the two. To date, this arrangement of courses has yielded gratifying results.

We thus have the means of providing the student of composition with a sound technique to enable him to handle with ease every style that may suit his personality.

We must now deal with aesthetics.

The aesthetics of each individual is evidently the result of his own reflections in the face of the attitudes of his several teachers, of his own musical environment, and even of society as a whole towards music. Whereas technique must be universal in character in that it should enable the student to feel at ease in any style or medium, aesthetics is pre-eminently *personal* since it must at all costs find a response in the *personality* of the composer.

But in spite of the individual character of the result, by his general attitude towards music and his manner of judging his pupil's efforts and of guiding him in his work, the teacher nevertheless has a preponderant influence on the shaping of the aesthetics of the budding composer. He therefore carries a heavy responsibility. In my opinion, it devolves upon him to counteract the all-too-prevalent attitude of seeking novelty for novelty's sake. Far be from me the thought of wanting to maintain art in general or music in particular in a more or less advanced traditionalism; but this frenzied super-innovation is decidedly unhealthy as well as irrational. The composer, who quite evidently no longer writes for his contemporaries, must remember all the same that music, like any other art, is a medium of communication. If he is not writing for today, he must be writing for the future.

Unfortunately, the novelty which he has so eagerly sought as an end in itself will have already grown old tomorrow, and the teacher must imbue his pupil with a sense of values of a perennial character. How right was he who spoke of "the classics, those moderns that endure," for a true work of art belongs both to its own time and to all times.

And this brings us, as in a circle, to where we were a while back: to find these perennial values, our principal tool will be acoustics, since it alone does not vary with whims, taste, style, period, or aesthetics.

To sum up, the future composer must study both traditional and present-day techniques, basing them on the definite data furnished by musical acoustics. The master under whose direction he works must inspire him with the necessity of basing his writings on stable values, free from the influence of changing fashions, presenting a character of universality and permanency. It is seldom necessary to emphasize to the gifted pupil the necessity of present-day musical thought. As to the ungifted one, he cannot be given gifts which he is lacking: only a born composer can be trained to become one.

[translated from the French by the author]

Aurelio de la Vega (CUBA)

The professional musician, the intelligent music lover, and, to a lesser degree, the perennially baffled general public that all through history has lived a century in retard, are lately more or less puzzled and amazed at the discovery that, after the Second World War, most of the music coming from Europe has been expressed in a totally new language. This language not only has a peculiar structure and sound in itself, but is written in a completely new symbolic language.

One of the most amazing facts about European culture is that it never ceases to produce, one way or another, the most daring, different, and profound artistic-aesthetic movements, and that even after a recent cataclysm such as the one that threatened to destroy whole nations, the roots of the millenary tree seem to keep alive, constantly producing new fruits. With few exceptions, starting with the illustrious Walt Whitman and up to the recent abstract expressionist paintings of the New York Group and some striking architects like Luis Candela, Frank Lloyd Wright, or Oscar Niemeyer, our American continent has not yet been able to produce strong enough and large enough artistic movements to balance, in their novelty and singularity, the continuous flux of events in Europe.

Precisely because music is the most abstract and usually the latest developed artistic aspect of any given culture, it is in this domain that the differences are more obvious. If we analyse both Americas, we will see that, with the possible exception of John Cage and Milton Babbitt, few things have been accomplished that could equal the originality of movements like the Schoenbergian twelve-tone technique axis and its immediate sequels: the Webern realm and the serially oriented generation of young European composers. And it is because of this extraordinary fact that we should consider in the Americas the necessity of a total reorientation of our technical approach to the craft of musical composition, since it is time that the evident scientific and technological awareness that characterizes other aspects of our culture be also applied in the domain of music.

In the years of the National-Socialist regime in Germany and the Fascist tenure in Italy, these two major countries suffered a total eclipse of their creative musical forces. Hindemith and Malipiero, for example, were names already belonging to the First World War generation, and their music, like that of many other composers, was banned for years in these countries. At that moment, let us say, at the beginning of the thirties England was, as usual, rather dormant, surrounded by the aural conceptions of the pompous Sir Edward Elgar; Russia was busy trying to shape the new plan and by-laws of Soviet realism; and France, still shocked by the barbarism of Stravinsky, placidly dreamed in the never-ending post-impressionist clouds. The real core of the most significant aesthetic revolution of our century, namely the tonal and structural reorientation of music as proposed by Schoenberg and his two illustrious pupils, was to be found in Austria, which, significantly, was one of the countries that suffered to a greater degree the consequences of Versailles. But the Schoenbergian revolt was to have a short European vogue at that time, for in 1934 we see Schoenberg taking refuge in America, and in 1935 we know of Berg's sufferings because of the difficulty in producing much of his music. The next ten years are going to witness the indomitable Webern secluded in his iron tower, not ivory, for this extraordinary man was to produce in total solitude his most splendid and courageous works.

During the Second World War only France, in the middle of the occupation and suffering the pains of the defeat, continued to be a relatively fertile ground for the development of the first rhythmically oriented serial ideas of Messiaen. In the meantime in America, the cult of Hindemith, the belated discovery of Bartók after his death, the typical Eastman style, the colouristic pranks of so many Latin American composers, and the nationalistic fever carried to extreme nonsense were innocuous achievements in our musical life. Everyone in this part of the world spoke glowingly about Prokofiev's lyricism and praised Shostakovitch's *Leningrad Symphony* as a masterpiece, obviously with the curious political overtones of that memorable era when Russia was still for the Western powers "our white dove." Nobody thought that the Schoenbergian world was suddenly to explode with an unprecedented force on the post-war European scene, and many were the musicologists, conductors, composers, music critics, and intelligent dilettantes who believed the nightmare of the twelve-tone Central European thirties was gone forever, and was to remain in the music text-books as an isolated and esoteric experiment. The impact of post-war European music on any serious-minded musician from the Americas was tremendous. For here, once more, that apparently exhausted culture had produced, in an amazingly short number of months, one of the most total, complete, and radical new art forms of our century. The isolation produced by the years of war mysteriously fused all the hidden implications of the Schoenberg-Webern binomial and a totally reshaped and new music made its appearance.

Serial music is not only a new technical approach to musical composition, but also a new philosophical concept of this art where the elements of time and space, as already stated by Webern, take a complete organic shape. Like every important movement in the history of culture, this music, which now covers all Europe and has already established beach-heads in the United States, comes accompanied with a new language that expresses itself with words which sometimes do not even seem to have relation with the art of music. We may discuss forever at gatherings, conferences, round tables, and panel discussions the so-called dehumanization of electronic music, and end these discussions with cries against this blasphemous new art. But no matter how much we dislike a thing, we must accept it the moment it becomes evident that its life and implications are not limited by a momentary fashion.

For example, one fact is evident at this stage of the musical picture of our century: that the return to traditional tonality, no matter how expanded and dissonant this may be, is absolutely impossible, and that, accordingly, the functions of the structure of music, its vocabulary, and even its symbolic meaning have to change radically. No serious-minded composer can escape the fact that the Schoenberg revolution destroyed traditional harmony, probably forever, and the subsequent post-Webern evolutions are the established and normal procedures of musical expression. With the isolated exception of Soviet Russia, whose political system has produced a music almost eighty years old and therefore unable to influence western European thought, no other major group of creators can escape nowadays these facts.

It is interesting to remember that the last major composer of our Occidental culture who represented the diatonic traditional system —namely Stravinsky—has finally accepted, after the early experiments of the *Canticum Sacrum* and *Agon*, the serial language. His last splendid work, the *Movements for Piano and Orchestra*, conclusively proves this point. Even an advocate of nationalism and "Americana" like Aaron Copland, has yielded in his *Fantasy* for piano to the early pressures of the time, and many composers from Latin America, whose music, even a decade ago, was couched in the most traditional language, are now twelve-tone composers. Of course, as is the usual case, we are always a little late in this part of the world to catch up, and we discover in America the twelve-tone procedures when these are already an academic subject in Europe. It is important to know, for example, that the Berlin Hochschule für Musik has a full year course in twelve-tone composition, something which we still consider too daring in our hemisphere. But our mild twelve-tone composers from America at least prove to us again that traditional harmony is a thing of the past, and the previous generation of Eastmanites in the United States has been superseded by the Webernites. By comparison, how venerable now seem Hindemith, Bartók, Milhaud, Honegger, or the Mahlerian utterances of some British and Soviet composers!

It seems clear that the development of harmony as we have traditionally conceived it has reached a dead end. Composers, after exhausting all the possibilities of vertical combinations, seem by and large no longer interested in chords as such. This is a tacit recognition that nothing is left to be discovered in the sphere of harmony that arouses any feelings of excitement. This does not mean, of course, that harmony has ceased to exist in any music, or that it has become an element to be ignored. Our harmonic sense is essentially the awareness of one of the dimensions of music, and, if art is to be developed, awareness of every aspect of the musical art must increase and change. But, as Sessions says, "harmonic effect as such has clearly ceased to be a major interest of composers, just as tonality has ceased to be a point of reference against which issues can be adequately discussed." Undoubtedly the focal point of the more advanced musical thought of today is polyphonic, and mainly concerned with problems of texture and organization instead of with harmony in the traditional sense of the word. Again, this does not mean that composers have ceased to be aware of vertical relationships, or progressions from one complex of sounds to another. But it is true that they tend more and more to think of these matters in terms of texture rather than in terms of regular harmony. This is why we see vertical conglomerates referred to as "densities" rather than as "chords."

Quite as important to remember is the fact that serialism is in full process of development, and that it is no longer the exclusive possession of any one "school" or group of composers, nor is it bound to any one mode of expression. In other words, it is a technical principle that a wide number and variety of composers have found useful for their own purposes, both because of the organizing principles they have derived from it and because of the musical resources it has opened up for them. As Richard Franko Goldman says, "music, up to now, like the physical time in which it exists, has been considered irreversible. Our understanding of harmony is of course based on this irreversibility. But with the popularization and distortion of notions of relativity, coupled with concepts of modern mathematics, it is perhaps now the conceit to make music reversible as well as discontinuous." This supposition explains the denial of harmony as an element of construction, which is basic in the post-Webern world.

It is thus evident that a great disparity exists between the reality forming our actual mode of composition and the teaching of music in our institutions, where the most traditional methods are often still employed. A mere glance through any of the important European musical publications convinces us that we are dealing with a totally new language in music. It is sufficient to read the excellent October, 1959 issue of the *Musical Quarterly*, which compiles all the papers read at the Princeton Seminar for Advanced Musical Studies, to understand that the new language of music has finally come to America, in many cases introduced by such eminent composers as Krenek or Sessions, in others as a final recognition of the previously obscure contribution of men like Schillinger and Babbitt. In reading these articles one is aware that, at least among our musical minorities, there exists a definite desire finally to bridge the eternal cleavage that has separated the Americas from Europe. This is one of the most important and touching consequences of the Princeton Seminar, which might well stand as a kind of incipient Darmstadt in our Western Hemisphere.

What is the exact state of affairs in our colleges and universities and in our conservatories of music in America? With an evident laziness tinted with fear, we blindly keep instructing our composition majors in the arts and ways of traditional harmony, a discipline that is usually spread over six semesters of instruction. Occasionally, in the most daring institutions, a special post-graduate course deals with Schoenberg, and hidden in some remote corner of our catalogues we find sometimes units given under Independent Studies headings, by which our most promising students bypass the traditional curriculum to undertake research on Webern or Stockhausen. At the end of their instruction, sometimes even when receiving a Master's degree, our students are suddenly faced with the reality that in the world of serious music nothing they have learned from a composition point of view is valid any more. In a way it is plain cheating, as if a student today would undergo a rigorous training in surgery only to be informed after the completion of his studies that the methods he learned were the ones used at the beginning of our century. It is true that this state of affairs is not the sole property of the Americas, since in such a respectable European institution as the Conservatoire de Paris Fauré's harmony is still conscientiously analysed, and the Wieniawski school of violin playing is still valid. But if we really want to tackle this situation honestly and produce the subsequent betterment of our cultural, technical, and musical resources, we should give some serious thought to the reorganizing and reorienting of the teaching of music.

One thing is evident in what we have been witnessing: profound and radical changes in the concept of music have taken place in our time. Such changes can be compared with the appearance of polyphony in the ninth century, or with the establishment of the major and minor systems in the early Baroque. Music evolves continuously, and the speed at which the spiral moves is faster every day. After centuries of refinement revolving around the physical laws of the tonal system we have finally discovered a new land and, the cycle completed, we are to start on a new exciting venture that will probably take a couple of centuries to exhaust itself again. It is interesting to note that we usually marvel at any biological change in nature and are ready to accept the splitting of the atom, interplanetary trips, or the non-validity of the old sacred laws of Newton. But, amusingly enough, even we professional musicians are somewhat reluctant to accept a totally new state of affairs in which the concepts of tonality, vertical relation, melody, production of sound, and instrumental devices have taken a totally different twist and represent things completely opposite to what they used to mean.

All this does not mean that the past should be suddenly ignored, and that our music students majoring in composition are not even to be told that Schubert existed. But we certainly should be realistic and ready to instruct our new generation in methods and concepts that deal with the active forces of music now operating in the world. Just as in our traditional curricula mediaeval harmony is almost a musicological research study and modal counterpoint is usually taught after the eighteenth-century counterpoint, so we must place traditional diatonic harmony in the same perspective; we must also train our instrumental students in the playing of this new music which sometimes they don't even suspect exists.

Of course we all know that a great majority of the music students that fill the schools of music in our institutions are not composition majors, but in many cases performers, music educators, and even musicians whose careers will be tied to the popular music field. This last case is the most peculiar one, since it is a well-known fact that the differences which started separating art music from popular music in the nineteenth century constitute by now an insurmountable abyss, to such an extent that the sound seems to be the sole common ground between the two. However, for the student who legitimately wants to earn a living with traditional music, regular courses in harmony, orchestration, arranging, and so forth should form part of the curriculum—as they should for the music educator, who will insist for many more years to come that the only way to teach music to a child is to play *The Moldau*, trying to count collectively in class the number of waves of the damned river.

But once these majorities are covered, what do we offer in our curricula to the serious music major in composition, or to the serious-minded performer? We must remember in this last case that much of our actual music has also produced, among other things, a totally new reorientation in the art of playing, and the basic techniques of the instruments must also be reshaped to accommodate the playing of new scales and phrases. In his book, *Conversations with Igor Stravinsky*, Robert Craft points out that with the exception of some specialist groups of players in New York or in Los Angeles many of our performers are placed in a disadvantageous position compared with their European colleagues, when playing the music of Boulez, Nono, Pousseur, and even Webern. It is remembered in Los Angeles that, when Stockhausen visited the city two years ago, he was unable to perform there his *Zeitmasse* because of the insufficient number of rehearsals. In the more socialized European systems, where the player is an employee of the state and earns the same salary whether he rehearses Beethoven's Ninth Symphony ten times or Boulez's *Improvisations sur Mallarmé* sixty-eight times, this encounter with new music is not as dramatic, because the playing of this type of composition on state radios and at numerous Festivals has acquainted him with the new art. In my own composition courses, for example, I often find students who are otherwise excellent players completely baffled and confused even with the counting of the rhythmic pulsations of most serial music. Since they will probably play this type of music only sporadically we should introduce in our curriculum special analytical courses that will deal with this state of affairs, thus producing, at the same time, a circular chain reaction with the subsequent interest of organizations and public in the performance of the music.

Finally it is also important to remember that our music history courses should deal more extensively with music composed after the Second World War. It is well known how heavily tradition weighs upon us and how difficult it is to introduce any major changes in our established plans of studies. Again as a personal experience, I remember that the recent introduction of a simple course devoted to the Music of the Americas, in our rather progressive San Fernando Valley State College, produced the most varied reactions from colleagues at many points in the United States, and to my astonishment I discovered that the course seems to be the only really organic attempt of its kind. Apparently most institutions have offered this type of course only sporadically, have concentrated their coverage only on the music of the United States, or have finally offered a brief vision of contemporary music in Latin America by some visiting professor from south of the border during a Summer Session.

In summary, I would like to say once more that I think it is time we condense our traditional harmony courses in one or two semesters, devoting considerably more time to the teaching of new concepts and tools, developing a sensitive ear for the new aural combination, creating a mental attitude suitable to the grasping of the new vocabulary, and encouraging a technical command of the instruments and the voice when confronted with the new media. To turn our backs on the electronic machines or the latest scores published in Europe is acting a little like the ostrich. This procedure, so current and common in our political dealings and our moral evaluations, has proved sufficiently dangerous and negative. With open minds and hearts we should face our "brave new world" and, with a sane smile and high anticipations, begin to live our actual lives more vitally, more intelligently, and more courageously.

Discussion

Oskar Morawetz (CANADA): Mr de la Vega, first of all I would like to tell you that Franz Kraemer, who unfortunately isn't here, but who studied with Alban Berg, once told me that somebody came to Berg and said he would like to study the twelve-tone system. Berg said, "That's fine; but I won't let you study it unless you study with me, for three or four years, traditional harmony. Otherwise I don't think you would understand it." You seem very clear what music is the music of the future and what is the music of the past. If it's as clear as you said, lots of composers would never have written a note of music. For instance why should Brahms have bothered to write anything—since he was born twenty years later than Liszt and used a language which was much more old-fashioned than Liszt himself? The funny thing is that after a hundred years nobody cares when the music was written but only how good the music is. If you are good in a style and have something personal to say, you can say something new in any language. The new things which you have brought up will in forty years be also old-fashioned, and what will remain is what the composer has to say personally—what is inspired, not what is new.

de la Vega: Our times in music, as in science, are very important revolutionary times. This is the first thing we should be aware of. The difference between Liszt and Brahms is not the same difference as between Max Reger and Webern, because this is a major change —a fundamental change in direction in the history of music, in which even the symbolic language is going to change, probably has already changed. Now the idea that you employ—"If it's good art it doesn't matter"—this is a rather difficult thing to accept because you could not point to one single masterpiece in the history of art which repeats the previous language and just stays there. It is interesting that you bring up, as is often done, as a kind of musical marvel, this question: Why is it that Schoenberg and Berg taught traditional counterpoint? I think they taught traditional counterpoint because at their moment they thought it was necessary for the bridging of the gap. I think this is no longer an important problem. We have left it behind, somehow. We are in a completely new land, and don't need any more this sort of going back and forth.

Papineau-Couture: Our positions are very near, but this is where we disagree: you say that Schoenberg invented a new *concept*. There is an element of new concept in Schoenberg; but there is mainly a new *technique*. Whatever there is of new concept you can find already in a composer who was named before by Dr Morawetz, that is, in Liszt. You can find it also in Wagner. Schoenberg merely developed the chromatic concept of Wagner into a new technique. The technique is very important to study as such, but it is not with technique only that we build a work—there is the conception of music, there is the aesthetics, and so on. This is why we need to study some academic subjects—I mean tonal harmony, counterpoint, and fugue; and when I say fugue I am ready to remind you that fugue is also a technique, which in many ways is akin to the twelve-tone system, and that a piece is not good just because it is a fugue—there must be something else that will justify a fugue on acoustic principles. This twelve-tone composer and that twelve-tone composer have very different ideas and you cannot say there is a fixed system. You have not here a neutral ground on which you can rely for the basic formation of a student. Of course he will need to know everything about the twelve-tone system, *afterwards*—when he has reached the point where he can understand what he is doing. But at first he does not understand what he is doing and the twelve-tone system is not a thing to teach you what you are doing—it is a thing which has to be learned later on.

de la Vega: A fugue is not a valid exercise any more; I think it's a museum type of thing. I don't think I should teach a student of mine to write a fugue, because he is wasting his time somehow. The new forms in music do not relate to this—this marvellous form, that was valid for centuries; I bow to it, but it is no longer valid. I should substitute for it something new, and later relate to the student the story of the fugue, as something that happened in the past.

COMPOSER AND PERFORMER

Václav Dobiáš (CZECHOSLOVAKIA)

In approaching the theme of today's discussion, the relationship between composer and performer, I should like to state briefly what this relationship is like in the Guild of Czechoslovakian Composers. During the first years of this organization's activity, it was made up of composers, musicologists, and critics only. But we have come to consider the performance of new works as our foremost task—which has meant, in the course of the last year alone, about eighty-eight concerts of contemporary music sponsored by our Guild (two-thirds being chamber music concerts and one-third orchestral concerts), not only in Prague but also where there are branches of our Guild, and elsewhere too. Thus close relationship with our performers has necessarily been established. Thus also, in 1955, the best Czechoslovakian performers became members of our Guild and our organization assumed its present structure.

The membership is approximately 750 and we have three sections: (*a*) the composers, with about 400 members; (*b*) the musicologists, with about 150 members; (*c*) the performers, with about 200 members.

Prospective members of our Guild must be professionally qualified. Composers and performers must have a music-school degree with high standing; musicologists and critics must have a university degree. This degree is no guarantee of acceptance for membership, for the decisive factor is the applicant's own creative work.

The members of the performers' section are active as soloists, conductors, and concert-masters in our symphony orchestras (there are eleven in our country, not including the radio symphony orchestras), or as soloists in our thirteen permanent opera houses, or as members of many of our best chamber music ensembles, such as the Smetana, Vlach, and Janacek Quartets. (Remember that Czechoslovakia today is a country of fourteen million inhabitants.)

The composers' section holds yearly, besides its regular concerts, what we call "Displays" of new works, that is, a series of concerts lasting a whole week. The performers' section has a similar "Display" week, enabling young performers to present themselves to the public in a festival of contemporary music. We must emphasize that the programmes of these concerts consist of contemporary music only.

After five years' practical experience, we find that the close link between composers and performers is of great value, and that it is practicable and most advantageous for composers and performers as well as for musicologists and critics. Belonging to a common family imposes on every member high ambitions, and this is all to the good.

It is a world-wide phenomenon that composers are no longer the best performers of their own works. Their medium is today, almost without exception, the performer. In comparison with us, the painter has the advantage that he needs no intermediary. Yet our disadvantage—that it is only the performer who gives life to our work—changes into our advantage: the musical work is given by him ever fresh beauty, so that it can live many lives.

Are the composers sufficiently aware of this advantage in working through an interpreter? Are we not transferring our complaints too much on to the performer—and frequently exclusively on to him?

The performer has the most lively contact with the public and he feels what is happening in a hall during a concert. The whole hall forms an entity with him when a good work is being played. The work provokes emotions which only music can give. The great masters—Bach, Mozart, Beethoven, and all the others—were constantly discovering new paths; they did not follow well-known ones. The same applies to great performers as well. In their courage they have spared no effort, no obstacles have deterred them. In this mission of theirs they have been guided by the most rigorous discipline and love for man. These artists have been and are creating for him, for his happiness. In the work of great artists lives not only man but also the whole of society, with its ideas of progress leading humanity ever further forward.

In this century, when technology has brought continents closer together, when the means of communication may reach, practically at the same time, people all around the world, it is (to say the least) strange how long various systems, such as quarter-tone music, electronic, serial, dodecaphonic, and concrete music, have been limited to a closed circle of people. Is it not reasonable to suspect that there is something not quite right in this music? And are we to blame the interpreter for these developments?

Our subject today is the relationship between the performer and the composer. But let us not forget that no-less-important figure, the listener. In his hands lies the destiny of music no less than in the hands of those who create it.

Gunther Schuller (USA)

I am a composer; but I am also a performer, and have been for many years—and, if I might say so myself very modestly, on a high level of performance, having played in the Metropolitan Opera orchestra for many years, and having also participated for all those years in performances of contemporary music in New York. So I feel that I can speak about the subject from both sides. One needs to speak not in generalities but about specific problems, which is what I should like to do. I should also like to speak specifically in relation to the problem of—well, what we have been calling serial music; because I think that this is where the real problem between the composer and the performer has been created.

I would like to make a plea—perhaps some of you will be surprised at this—a plea to the serial composer to take into consideration the innate, intrinsic characteristics of the instruments for which he is writing. We hear a lot of talk these days about how composition is becoming more and more wedded to the specific sonic material. Lip-service is paid to this all the time; and yet we hear pieces in which things are asked of the performers which go against that principle. So if I were to reduce this plea to a nutshell it would sound like this: if you are writing for instruments to be played by human beings, then take those into consideration and make those a part of your compositional material, and do not go against that material. If you feel that the human being, the human instrumentalist, is limiting you—well then, write for other means, possibly electronic means. But do not force the player into a kind of suspended position where he—and many of them try to do their very best with such pieces—where he is unable to give you what you really want. It is just not within the means of human beings to do some of the things which composers have been asking performers to do.

Now, I said I would be specific. I would like to name some names and some compositions. I happen to feel that Luigi Nono is one of the finest composers of my generation, or of our time. He's that great a composer because he has a certain lyric and expressive gift (with all his total serial organization); this lyric gift, which springs from a truly Italianate temperament, shines through the music. And yet the curious fact is that his music is great despite the way he actually writes for the instruments. By that I mean that he writes virtual impossibilities; and I've argued this with him personally for years. He is, by the way, not a performer in any sense; he does not play any instrument, not even the piano—so that he composes out of the personal vision that he has of music; but this vision ignores the performer to a large extent. He writes things which are virtually impossible; and what happens is that you get a performance which may be very exciting but is not exactly what the man wrote. You get a kind of transposition into human terms of the abstraction which is presented on the page. Now I don't know whether this is the future of music—it may be, we don't know—this is all too new. But I'd like to think that it is not, and as long as we have electronic means for realizing the stupendous difficulties that are demanded in such pieces as Nono's *Canto sospeso* or the *Varianti*, then why not use those means? Why continue this kind of sham of writing one thing and getting in performance another thing, and then saying that the two are the same?

Another instance was a piece which I heard recently in Cologne. It was by Pierre Boulez, who is another great composer, and yet he also has found himself in this trap of writing things which are literally impossible. For years, performers used to feel that the music of Webern and Schoenberg was *practically* impossible, but now I think that some composers have found a way of writing things which *are* impossible. Boulez had a section in this piece which consisted of two pages of uninterrupted thirty-second notes for about twenty instruments, and the speed at which these thirty-second notes went was something quite fast, like this [*tapping*]. Now this went on for two pages; it was quite long. The fact was, and I had it substantiated both by talking to the performers and by looking at the parts myself (and believe me, I'm not "chicken" when it comes to playing contemporary music; I like to get my teeth into anything that is challenging and demanding)—but the fact was that this piece was not playable as the man wrote it. And it wouldn't have made any difference if he wrote it in eighth notes instead of thirty-second notes: the speed with which these notes passed, and the intervals that were demanded, going from one thirty-second to the next, were just not possible, I would say, on half of the instruments which he wrote this for. So again, what happened? We had a grand noise, which was a kind of improvised music, but which was not what he wrote.

Pierre Boulez might say to me, of course, "Well, I *wanted* that improvisation; I only used that written page as a kind of stimulus to get this effect, which I cannot get any other way." At that point, I can no longer answer him. But I do not know whether everyone would take that view; and it's for those who would not that I'm making this point.

I'm not absolving the performer from having been for a great amount of his time delinquent in his duties in performing contemporary music. We all know the complaints we get from performers. Sometimes they are sincere; a lot of the time they are not, because performers often seem to be inherently lazy and against the new. To some extent we have to put up with this. When I speak of the performer, then, I'm speaking only of those who are sincerely interested and who have the technical ability to do most of what is being demanded today.

We mustn't forget that the middle-man between us and the consumer is the performer; and it is a fact, I think, that performance of contemporary music is much more crucial, much more important, in terms of getting the idea of the composition across, than performances of romantic, classical, or any other kind of music. Because, if we hear a bad performance of a Schubert symphony, all of us know this piece well enough to know that that was a bad performance, and in fact we can substitute for the bad spots and say, "Ah, yes, well, it's supposed to go like that." The piece is therefore not affected, because you know *a priori* what it was supposed to sound like. But when you hear a Webern or a Boulez or a Stravinsky piece for the first time you are at the mercy of the performer. When you hear a piece *of your own* for the first time, for that matter, you are also at the mercy of the performer. So it behoves you to be very careful in writing something that the performer can really, honestly, perform.

You have to analyse what kind of performer you are dealing with. If he's a bad performer, or one who shows antagonism or no interest, of course, then his doubts wouldn't prove you wrong. But if you are dealing with the finest performers, and if they tell you, "Well, look—this is just not possible, or if it is possible, it certainly will not give you the kind of result you want"—then we as composers should on occasion listen to them. When I spoke of the Boulez and Nono performances, I should have added that the performers in both instances were the finest available. The Baden Baden orchestra, which performed the Boulez piece, for instance, is probably the orchestra most adapted to playing contemporary music. They have come to grips with all the problems that have arisen. If *these* men say to a composer, "It's not possible"—then the composer, I think, must listen.

Victor Feldbrill (CANADA)

You've heard that the performer is a middle-man. The conductor is almost a double middle-man, because he is not only the link between the composer and the public; he must also be the link between the composer and the orchestra, and then add the public. (Believe me, there are some very gruesome hours sometimes before his function is completed.) I want to deal specifically with the problem of the orchestral player. I don't feel it is my place to say anything about the performer on the piano or the string or wind soloist; but until a few years ago most of my bread and butter was earned from playing within the orchestra and not outside it, so this is from practical experience.

As you must all very well know, and I think this is fairly well a universal problem, rehearsal time is always at a premium. There is rarely enough rehearsal time allotted for a new work. I do believe that you as composers can help us as performers a great deal if there are certain things you make sure of before the music arrives at a first rehearsal. The things I'm going to say may be quite obvious—but I have found in many instances that what I thought was obvious was not obvious to you as composers.

First, we must have clear manuscript. You cannot expect players to go through a rehearsal with music which they cannot read. Even more important—and this is squarely your duty and not the duty of a performer—correct your manuscripts before we get them. God knows, it's difficult enough to hear the right notes when they are right; it's much more difficult to hear them when they are wrong. Very often, and this is something else I would like to touch on, some of you have your music duplicated in certain processes—where, for example, the paper is blue and music is blue on top of that. Now this is a fact; and I might caution, if I may, our Russian colleagues here, that this is most true of their music. With my own orchestra, in Winnipeg, I've had great problems in performances of works of Shostakovitch and Prokofiev for the simple reason that the manuscript which we get is impossible to read. (If you will take that back, as a message, I would appreciate it.)

My colleague, Mr Schuller, has already mentioned the fact that Boulez wrote a composition in which there were two pages of thirty-second notes. Rehearsing this week for a Conference concert, we had, not pages, but a number of lines of thirty-second notes, which could just as easily have been eighth notes with the time-value indicated on the top; these would have been much easier for the performers to play. As it was, we managed to get over the hurdle, and, as you know, the players which we had here this week were an excellent group and we had no real problems after we got started. But there is a way of making things a little easier for the performer. If the piece is going very quickly, please make the stems and bar-lines as few as possible.

Another thing that is common in contemporary music is the composition with continual time-changes, where every bar is different. Now I know that there is a definite purpose for this; and I also know, from experience, that as far as the ear is concerned it does not know the difference if the orchestral player is given something written in 4/4 time rather than a series of short eighth-note bars. If the player is allowed to accent off-beats, the ear (I'm convinced) will pick up the same rhythm and have the same impulse.

Difficulty is governed by the speed of the composition: if it's very slow it doesn't matter that you have 5/8—4/8—3/8, etc.; but if it's going very quickly the orchestral player is at a great disadvantage, no matter how much rehearsal time he has for the work, because he is continually in the grips of having to count, and when he is counting he is tense, and when he is tense his reaction is slower, as you know, and things don't come off as you expect. So, to help yourselves, again I ask you to help the performer. Make it as easy for him as possible. I'm not asking you to write easier notes: I'm asking you to simplify your time-signatures, which will give you exactly the same results.

These remarks, of course, I have passed on for those of you who obviously in some cases (and I'm not saying this as a criticism) have never played in an orchestra. There's quite a difference between playing in an orchestra and perhaps sitting down and playing a sonata of your own. We have the problem of having sixty to a hundred (or even only eighteen) players responding in a fraction of a moment.

I will make another request of you which has been made already: take professional players into your confidence. They are not against you. They are only against you when you have given them problems which they cannot overcome, and when they feel that you don't think about what happens to them when they are playing. Take them into your confidence. And when I say professional players I don't mean, by any means, conductors—I mean the players in the orchestra; because a great number of *conductors* have not been orchestral players and themselves are not aware of these problems.

Mr Schuller made a plea, and I'm also going to make a plea to you. I had a very unusual experience this week for the first time, and if it indicates a growing tendency, then I'm a little afraid of the future of music as far as the human performer is concerned. I was asked specifically by one of the composers not to become emotionally involved with the music that we were performing. I would answer: if we, as performers, cannot become emotionally involved in what we are playing—and I don't mean emotions in a saccharine sense, but just emotions, any kind you want—then your audience will never become emotionally involved. I make this plea: if you want music that has no emotional involvement, I beg you to write for the electronic instruments; I'll be in the audience listening, but rather glad I won't have to perform.

Discussion

John Weinzweig (CANADA, *chairman*): Now there are a few minutes remaining—in which we can *all* become emotionally involved.

Guillermo Espinosa, conductor, and music director for the Pan American Union in Washington, raised an objection to composers' taking pride in the difficulty—or impossibility—of their music. He quoted a Venezuelan composer who boasted to him, a propos a violin sonata he'd just completed, that it "was so difficult even Heifetz couldn't play it."

Murray Adaskin (CANADA): I suggest we might give more consideration to writing pieces for junior players in our contemporary idioms. I have found that performers are trained to a too advanced stage by their teachers knowing absolutely nothing about the new techniques demanded of performers in this new music. We might help this situation considerably if we devoted a little of our time to writing first- to fourth-grade pieces for children. This may sound simple, but actually it's an interesting challenge and would help our cause enormously.

Jean Papineau-Couture (CANADA): I believe we'll soon have to have another conference, with the sole object of discovering what notation will best accommodate the rhythmic ideas of our era. For many centuries, we've had a system of writing down our music which is essentially binary—the whole note divides into two half-notes, the halves into two quarter-notes, and so on. There is only a limited ternary possibility through the use of the dot after the note, dotted notes being divisible normally into three; however, the new value obtained by this division is *not* dotted, and I can't divide it into three without the use of an artificial device, the triplet. For a long time things functioned very well, because musical thought was conditioned by this very system of writing. But at the present time composers evidently have had enough of this system conditioned by the division into two and the limited division into three. The division into five is now introduced which is totally opposed to the system. And we mustn't think the division into five is an abnormal, inhuman thing; it's found everywhere in nature, even more frequently than the divisions into two or three—consider the starfish, among many other examples. Apart from five, there are the other divisions—into seven, eleven—which one can run across. But all these require, with our present system, refinements that are extremely complex. This means the composer has to *reconsider* something that is in a complex ternary division, or in divisions of five or seven; he comes face to face with a problem in *écriture;* he must find a written form for his thoughts, one which is capable of being read by an executant—and this may involve many artifices.

I think it's clear that we need to invent a new system of notating rhythm. If every one invents a new system of his own, no good will come of that, because there won't be a general currency of any one system. We need an international assembly to deliberate this problem and to find at least the beginnings of a solution. Executants, composers, and theorists should be invited; soloists too: if soloists play few new works, it's simply because the complexities, not of execution but of reading facility and rhythmic exactness, demand amounts of time they don't possess; a new system would make it easier for them just to *read* the works of their contemporaries. Once a new system is established I believe everyone will take the pains to study it (let's forget those who inevitably will want to remain in the past system). A new rhythmic system awaits discovery; we owe it to ourselves to work towards it.

An observer (USA): I associate myself with all Mr Papineau-Couture has said; all except his point of departure, which seems to me to demand some qualification. He traced the history of rhythmic structure, and here I have to object that the essential premise is the sense of symmetry, the sense of the *repeatability* of music. Now, this sense is absolutely lacking in most modern music. Mr Papineau-Couture calls for a new system of rhythmic notation to correspond to the inventions of modern composers; but this is going to be extremely hard. Think of the rhythmic practices of the great renaissance madrigalists—in an era when music was free of symmetry, of repeatability. As you know, there are two systems currently of transcribing, say, a Palestrina madrigal: one which strives in each line, each part, for the ideal logical sense of that part, so that the metre may change for each phrase; and another where a single metre is adopted for all voices, making of the rhythm little more than a convention, since it does not dictate accent, commencements of phrases, and so on. I'm deeply persuaded that in modern music one could arrive at a more easily comprehended result without changing metre so often. Rather than the divisions into nine and seventeen, I prefer a basic 3/4 metre in which, however, all minute changes of expression and phrasing are carefully shown. Does the composer sometimes adopt purposely the more complex forms of notational expression just to *épater* his executant? Let's recommend composers try to find the most simple, not the most complex, forms of notation.

Schuller: We're all oversimplifying now. There's a difference between a passage written in a succession of 3/8, 5/16, 11/32, or whatever, and a transformation of all of that into 4/4. The difference is that if you put it into 4/4 and place accents in keeping with the original notation, *you get syncopation.* If you play it in the original you do *not* get syncopation; you get emphases of strong beats and weak beats—an entirely different thing. The 4/4 transformation is not the solution. It *is* the solution in pieces written by third-rate composers who do not think through the rhythm carefully enough. The last parts of *The Rite of Spring* must be written in some kind of asymmetrical metric notation. Stravinsky himself has simplified it from the original, but it is still basically asymmetrical. Putting it all in 4/4 would give a very curious syncopated feeling which is not what the man intended.

Now, I agree our notation is hopelessly inadequate in many ways. But let's be realistic. We're dealing with a problem today, and it may be a century before we can work out another notational system, and the fact is that it *is* possible to realize today's compositional problems within our notational system; the composer only has to be a little more careful, perhaps also more learned. The problem is not in *reading* the notation, but rather in putting it into an instrument, in realizing it physically. We know how five or seven may be divided; the problem is to feel this so that it comes out resembling the music the composer intended. Notation after all is only a starting-point. The composer himself so often has not felt or "heard through" the rhythm that he is writing; he may well write a five because it looks fancy and *au courant*, whereas if he were forced to recite or play that rhythm he might be a lot more cautious about using it. And lest you think I'm now becoming the voice of reaction, I'll add that I believe that even in the most extreme, totally serialized music there is a reality possible for the performer.

Karl-Birger Blomdahl (SWEDEN): Surely any work of art should be as deep, as true, and as simple as possible. But in order to be true I cannot simplify. Might it not be that in order to be true I have to be complicated? *Then* I think the complication is perfectly justified. For me, if I write challenging, complicated things for instrumentalists, even if it's the utmost I can ask of an instrumentalist, this is much better than, as is so common nowadays, for instance, asking a violinist or a whole string section only to play above the bridge, or pluck the string in a way that may well spoil the string, or tap the back of the violin, knock it with the nails or hand—such things have nothing to do with the training of a fine musician.

Part Two
The Composer's Métier

SERIALISM

Iain Hamilton (GREAT BRITAIN)

I am sure that many composers today would agree with me that a separate discussion of serial music is somewhat dangerous. It suggests that it is some other form of composition and that its problems are something apart. In 1960 few would deny the validity and power of music which is not tonal. If one fails to accept the great new forces of our time, one is not actually living in our time. If one seeks to ignore or ridicule such great forces as the struggle for racial equality or communism, or if one fails to acknowledge to oneself that we live in an atomic age and that much of our thought and life is bound to be conditioned by it— if we bypass these real issues and developments then we lose the stimulation of our age. Whether we are in agreement with what has resulted from these forces, or how they have been managed, is another matter and of less importance than the fact that we should recognize them for what they are. Acceptance of, but not necessarily capitulation to, such great forces implies courage and an open mind. From such an acceptance could follow a possibility that the best results might be encouraged. But in saying that, I presuppose a great many things amongst which open-mindedness and a true enthusiasm for new ideas are not the least important. Since we observe just such a great force in the creative musical thought of our century, I shall deal in this paper with what seems to me to be the crux of the problem of creative musical thought today. I shall deal with no great technicalities or obscurities but try to show you how I, personally, feel that the great forces set in motion by Schoenberg, and developed by Webern, have done more than anything to face squarely the great dilemma which exists in music today.

The problem facing the artist in any age is basically how he will be able to resolve his imaginative power with form, a form which must be reborn and redeveloped unceasingly. No one saw this problem more clearly at any time than did Schoenberg during those crucial years which opened this century. The old regime at that time was toppling on all sides after having run a long and magnificent course. His complete understanding of all that went before him in the stream of Western music is evident in his tonal works, but no less in his theoretical writings which stand alone in their mastery. On the basis of this knowledge he took a resolute stand against the anarchy and exploitation of debased creative musical standards which followed the First World War. His stature, both as imaginative artist and as logical thinker in music, is now no longer denied, much as it may still be misunderstood. It is natural that composers such as Bartók, Stravinsky, and Hindemith should have been more readily accepted and assimilated at first as they are at once more obviously related to the past, as far as aural experience is concerned, because of their adherence to tonality. They sum up periods, however, and open up very little of consequence that is really vital and seminal. We have only to notice the effect that they have had on their copious followers. Their over-all use of bitonal harmonic structures, Hindemith's forced theory of harmony, Bartók's nationalism, chromaticism, and canonic imitation, Stravinsky's remarkable use of ostinati and obtrusive rhythm—all these diverse elements are fertile and resourceful in their own work maybe, but are really small matters in the solution of the great problems which confront us, compared with the steps taken by Schoenberg and Webern during the same period to grapple with the true problems of total polyphony and non-tonal sound structure. It has been the responsibility of our century to restore to music some of its dignity after the subservience to the other arts which it had known during the latter half of the nineteenth century.

Why then do I feel that we are in the process of restoring to music some of the great power at least that it had as music before the dreadful inclusiveness of the Romantic era? I shall try to show that many things are being reassessed and tackled boldly; only time can prove whether any of these will eventually be found of any consequence in the stream of creative music as a whole.

We have accepted, really only fully within the last decade, the fact that music need not be governed by the force of tonality. Although this was first recognized by Schoenberg half a century ago, the real influence of his work and thought is now finally ascertained. Young composers now accept these matters at the outset of their creative work; many other composers have come to accept them through their experience in tonal music. A certain intoxication is felt and no less a sense of responsiblity.

Tonality once rejected, one is faced with the need to rethink certain fundamentals of one's art. Each composer must find his own solution. Schoenberg, even in his greatest serial works, adhered to basically classical forms, although in the late *String Trio* and in the *Violin and Piano Fantasy* there are interesting developments as regards form of quite another kind. It is in the work of Webern, however, that we sense, even from his earliest work, a determination and an ability to create a new thinking about form and an execution of this form in relation to the ideas and technique involved. Complete polyphony is achieved in the work of Webern as it had hardly ever been achieved since the sixteenth century. The whole of the classical system of thought and technique is dispensed with except for what is essential to any work of art in any period. A reassessment of these essentials in relation to one's own work is one of the great challenges of our time. A true appreciation of late Debussy, as well as many fruitful developments in the work of Stravinsky in all his periods, has shown clearly that the trend is to move nearer and nearer to an attitude of music as music. Musical problems have to be thought out in musical, as opposed to philosophical or literary, terms. We have also escaped from the tyranny of the theme and the overpowering sublime ideas and ideals of the Romantics. Much as we may enjoy a certain amount of this music, we cannot but admit that too often it submits to the tyranny of the other arts. In this century a new musical unity has been achieved between horizontal and vertical; it may still be in early stages of development as regards a long period, but there is something positive about it which is stimulating.

Left then with our resources limited but ennobled as regards music, how shall we align these strictures with the great variety within unity which all art must possess? As we no longer consider tonality to be the overriding power, it is no longer logical to employ those forms, sonata, rondo, and fugue, which rely for their true meaning on it. As we no longer, therefore, have these forms it is equally invalid to think in terms of the symmetries which they condition. Webern was quick to realize this in his use of pre-classical polyphonic devices with their emphasis on smaller and momentary symmetry, rather than on larger and over-all symmetry.

Bereft of these elements I doubt if any really creative composer is very much hindered or dismayed. One is stimulated by the need to reappraise such basic elements as variation, texture, density, recapitulation, dynamics, instrumentation, etc. Such fundamentals have been the real concern of creative musicians during the last decade whether they have used electronic or purely musical means. Their concern, in other words, has been to reorganize the means whereby a composer can express his ideas and imagination. The rejection of the great classical line and the over-evident stream of melody, while not yet complete in Schoenberg, is wholly so in Webern and in such composers as Stockhausen and Boulez. Yet no one would deny these composers a definite line in their works. It is a newly conceived line, conceived with a new attitude to symmetry, recapitulation, and variation. Even in a pointillist score such as Nono's *Canto Sospeso*, one is not blind to the underlying line which after all must be there or the music can have no logic at all. All these terms such as pointillism and fragmentism, and the fascination for the isolated note, have blinded only the over-fanatical and the underexperienced to the true linear quality of this music.

Another important reassessment has been that accorded to the elements of improvisation, and even chance. This ranges from the *tachiste* use of both elements in the work of John Cage to the much more consciously integrated and ordered use of it in Stockhausen and Boulez. In the *Klavierstück 11* and *Zyklus* for percussion of Stockhausen both elements are employed, highly organized material being played in a more freely conditioned manner including the element of chance as far as selection goes. In the *Zeitmasse* of Stockhausen and Boulez's *Mallarmé Improvisation no. 2*, however, one sees how the element of improvisation can be ordered to give to the music a quality of fantasy within the strict technique of composition. These works, in fact, in entirely different ways re-establish the role of the arabesque and of the fioritura—elements of an essentially melodic nature. The emphasis too often on the *tachiste* application of the element of chance must not blind us to the wholly fruitful effect it may yet have if used sincerely.

I am personally greatly concerned with the rethinking of form in all its manifestations. I divide my works into very short sections which are valid only in so far as they bear the closest and most logical relation to one another. Each must complement, reinforce, and even comment on the other and in this way I try to find a unity and variety at the same time; this must exist if the sections are to be more than mere sections. Material and its presentation, density and the selection of instruments from the whole orchestra or group employed, texture and variation of tempo—all these elements are brought under constant review and development as I work. One seeks to achieve a symmetry which will be valid in relation to the work in question without being in any way pedantic or too preconceived. Texture can be variously worked with in layers and an infinite variety becomes available to one in yet another way, which is further proof of how rich and untrammelled is this whole world of sound once one has passed beyond tonality. The element of musical experience is manifested in a new way, material being heard in different versions and in different relationships, at various stages of the work. In the classical period this was never better achieved than when, in the recapitulation section of sonata form, the original material is heard again much as before except for key change, after our experience of it in the development section during which it has undergone great and often dramatic change.

It is no longer possible to think of harmony in any way approximating that used in tonal forms. Fluctuating density and varied polyphony free the mind and replace anything as rigidly ordered as chords, and particularly inversions. The pre-classical hearing by interval, both vertically and horizontally, is substituted and music again becomes contrapuntal in thought and execution. Therefore, although many of the classical formulae are abandoned, the deeper entities of music of any period or style are still observed but are rethought and reapplied as befits a new conception of sound and music.

Nothing has been so boringly debated and written about as the serialization of music, complete or partial. Such matters are only of any worth in discussion between two composers each with a personal point of view and if the music of each is known to the other. Each composer fights his own personal battle here and it is really his own personal concern. Those who find some new twist and get up and lecture to us about it, before we have heard a note of the music concerned, are apt to be tedious and are usually worse. Because of a certain amount of this posturing, which is no doubt inevitable at any time in the history of the arts, one again and again hears the most fatuous arguments put up against serious composers meeting this challenge honestly by writing good works. Any composer must find some means to organize his ideas and imagination without which he can hardly claim to be a creative artist at all. No technique evolved in our time has been so resourceful as some development of that initiated by Schoenberg. Many composers have found ways to deal with the unruly and vague situation as they found it, but none evolved in his work anything comparing favourably with the great logic and resource of the classical system, unless it be that of Schoenberg and his followers. Few who have not used it are aware of its possibilities, and I have never heard more nonsense talked about anything, by men who ought to know better, than when ill-informed and arrogant musicians talk about serial technique. It is neither easier nor more difficult to use than any other, neither does it automatically produce more interesting work. It has to be in the hands of a real composer and, as I said at the start, this division into serial and non-serial is dangerous.

There may be many composers who worked at an earlier stage of their development in a tonal style yet who found that certain elements of organization multiplied in their thinking and led them almost unaware, or even reluctantly, to some form of serial technique. This increased organization, limitation, and consequently economy will not hinder a creative composer, as his force must be trammelled in some way if his ideas are to mature and be distilled to give their true worth. The furious force is directed through an increasingly critical and selective channel, which more and more casts out what is prolix and too effusive. Only a weak force can be the worse for this purging process. It is impossible to judge one's own talent but one can judge how one uses it, and such a technique either liberates or constricts. He who finds himself constricted by it must leave it alone and find some other way.

A fatal way seems to me to be compromise between tonal and non-tonal. Admittedly Stravinsky has managed this very well in several of his most recent works but this is but a further example of this great and unique man being able to absorb anything into his style without in any way changing from his basically tonal foundations. Those who follow him into these dangerous waters find themselves where they have always found themselves when they have come too near this fatal flame. One comes upon many so-called serial works which have a basically classical form, a bass line pacing about in octaves, and a reassuring tonal pole on almost every page. Such a pseudo-serial approach seems as pointless as any other compromise where serious artistic problems are concerned. Britten's use of series in his recent *Cantata Academica* and in his new opera, *A Midsummer Night's Dream*, is, more correctly, an excellent example of a further organization of tonality than any attempt to work in a world of sound divorced from its shackles. This gives to these two works a remarkable lucidity even for Britten and enlarges his tonal range, but it is in this way that one must assess it and not as any new facet of serial technique.

Once aware of the infinite possibilities open to him in the new world of sound, the composer may often feel, as I said before, intoxicated. A real composer is never in need of a gimmick, but I doubt if there have ever been more in operation than during the last few years. These will, however, be eventually forgotten as the musical Dadaisms of the twenties have passed away and we now value from that period the initial developments of serial technique in the work of Schoenberg, Berg, and Webern and the work of Stravinsky.

Apart from such composers as Stravinsky and Britten today, what then is there that shows anything like the logical development towards something as positive as the abandoned classical system? For whether we like it or not we are in a world of sound no longer governed by the laws of tonality. One hears a great deal of music, long symphonies, concertos, and chamber works written in a kind of debased classical tonality, or worse, in a kind of shapeless free-chromatic limbo. One realizes that a composer may pass through a period of the composition of some such works at a certain stage of his development, but it seems strange that a composer can be content to remain in what is surely a dead world. I also find it strange that one composer should be content to use another composer's hard-won style and feel no responsibility that he must contribute something of his own if he is to meet the challenge offered to him. In this I sense a kind of arrogant unwillingness to accept, and to come to terms with, one's time without in any way compromising; I feel it to be an attitude of fear.

One cannot say what will come of all these developments—that is not our task. Great figures such as Stravinsky and Britten may continue to find resource in the tonal world. Yet one must not forget that they have accepted elements of serial thinking into their tonal world. In fact it is no longer possible to consider that any important new manifestation of tonality could take place without being affected in some way by non-tonal or serial tendencies. That alone is indeed some measure of the force of Schoenberg's evolution.

I am not so unrealistic as to imagine that all music can at once function satisfactorily in a serial technique. Entertainment music will, I imagine, for a long time retain its tonal basis, for I find no pleasure in the confusion of attitudes which might impel me to waltz or samba to serial dance music. The creative artist must, however, do more than entertain; he must, among other things, grapple with his immediate inheritance. One is more concerned with what one is bequeathed by one's father than with what one's father is bequeathed by one's grandfather. It will interest us, but concern us less. How many there are who are still quite unaware of their immediate musical inheritance and, in consequence, are unaware of the riches afforded them by that great inheritance!

George Rochberg (USA). *Duration in Music*

Any discussion of duration in music must necessarily probe the nature of duration itself, particularly as it relates to human experience. Without even the most limited understanding of the relationship between duration and existence, it becomes virtually impossible to comprehend how music becomes the living, dynamic, artistic embodiment of time; for music's great power over all men fundamentally derives from the engagement of the sense of duration in the listener, perceived as motion and movement, the occurrence of successive events which culminate in a sense of fullness of experience, of a sonorous content whose passage in time is rich and meaningful.

How do we perceive duration in life? We, as sentient beings for whom the external world provides a multitude of changing visual and aural stimuli, come to learn that nothing stays for us, nothing remains the same; we and the world around us move on in a continuous chain of events. As Rilke says in his *Duino Elegies*: "Once for everything, once only. / Once no more. / And we, too, once. / And never again." The present, the only moment in which we know we exist, is burdened by the weight of accumulated past experience; and the future is always one moment ahead, one moment ahead of us, the next "present" moment in which we hope to exist. So we live between memory and anticipation, between the past and the future, treading the bridge of the present which we hope will carry us across. Duration becomes for us the inexorable passage of time which nothing can hold back. We live in time and through time. We are both of it and immersed in it. The present is therefore more than the moment of physical existence in which we feel pain or joy, in which we experience our lives as something or nothing. It is destined to join the vast accumulation of all the other lived moments of life, all the other somethings or nothings. It will soon become the past just as it is already eroding the future.

The dynamic of duration is not only change but growth through change; for in this procession of ephemeral moments nothing is lost, nothing is left behind because everything becomes a part of memory whether consciously or unconsciously so. The past is reclaimed by memory and it is only by means of this act of reclamation or conservation of lived experience that a human being can come to know himself. Without memory he has no history, his life has no form. He would live only in the sensation of each passing moment, remembering nothing of what has occurred, unable to anticipate anything ahead. Life as we know it would be lost to such a being, condemned to exist in such a void, without memory of his former inner states and without the power to project their continuance into an anticipated future. His existence would be lost in the meaninglessness of each sensation. A mental life, affective and reflective in nature, must know the modes of duration— past, present, and future, in order to retain its identity and uniqueness.

There is no apparent form to the succession of our lived moments. As duration flows in an unbroken stream, events occur without plan, unforeseeable and unpredictable. If they are to have any pattern of meaning for us we must mentally sort and arrange them according to our ideas of order. Affective memory alone, re-living or re-feeling the past, cannot do this for us. We need the power of critical reflection in order to shape to our purpose what has taken place. We literally must impose an order of some kind on our affective memory if we are to see meaning in our existence. It is in the power of forming the data of our existence that we shape ourselves and the world around us; and it is out of this power, this urge to meaning through form and order that art arises. All our arts derive then from the interpenetration of the modes in which we experience life in the phenomenal world. All the forms of art correspond in some way to our need for or idea of order and project through sensuous material the modes of our existence in forms we can comprehend. Through music we experience, outside of ourselves and outside of those events in life which have a purely personal connotation, duration itself; but not in an absolutely pure sense. Just as in ordinary existence the sense of the passage of time comes to us through the perpetually shifting phenomena of the external life which surrounds us, so in music we sense the passage of time through the sensuous data of sound, formed as sonorities, melodies, and harmonies, constantly moving from shape to shape and point to point. In the listener is evoked a direct intuitive response because he knows by his intuition that this is the way life is too—with the important exception that music comes to him as form, while life does not. Music engages his sense of duration because duration is the primary condition of music.

This engagement of the listener's sense of duration calls his faculty of memory into direct play. Just as memory preserves his personal, unique past, it now makes possible the recognition and remembrance of musical ideas which he has already heard as the music unfolds itself to his mind and ears. Even though the music to which he is listening is already formed, the listener must re-create this form in his own mind in order to grasp it. Repetition and return in music therefore function as important and fundamental formal aspects of composition. If like the existence Rilke describes—"Once for everything, only once. / Once no more. / And we, too, once. / And never again"—music too should go on offering one new idea after another, aural sensation after aural sensation without repetition or return, it would lose itself in its own moments and therefore lose its form. Though "return" in music is seemingly like the recall of memory of lived human experience, it is not precisely analogous. Life is never a closed form because we do not know what death is; but music is necessarily a closed form. Ideas do come back in music to be heard again. In life only our memory of past moments can bring back their flavour and quality. Memory is affective, mental. The past may be re-called or re-felt but only internally. It cannot be physically experienced a second time. Return or recall in music is actual, that is, like the idea of which it is either a literal repetition or varied recall, it is *there*, physically present as sound. Nevertheless we can see powerful connections between the phenomenon of human memory of lived experience and return in music. In life, memory centres on those moments and events which have for the subject meaning in terms of the uniqueness of his existence. These memories are the substance of his life. Without them, as we have noted, he would have no mental or affective life other that what passed through him as feeling each moment of his existence. Analogously recall or return in music establishes the necessary condition for the meaning of the music experienced as formal order in and through duration. What the composer repeats or recalls must necessarily have meaning. The listener corroborates this by the degree to which he is able to recreate the form of the music.

Return in music then must have the same power to affect as does memory in life. It must be sharply evocative and yet quite literally occur in the present tense as though what is experienced in memory is again experienced in the present moment of life. The power of return in music serves much more than a purely formal function about which we have heard so much in the past from theorists and aestheticians: ideas of unity in variety, variety in unity, repetition and return creating formal unity, etc. This is merely a mechanical description of how perceived repetition and return affect a musical form. It does not account for the sheer power of return nor does it account for the enormous satisfaction gained when the meaning of a work is suddenly crystallized by the arrival at ideas stated earlier in a work emerging on a new plane. Return in music has something of the force of the past suddenly illuminating the felt present as a real element in the present. This suggests the possibility that music is an attempt, limited by human finitude, but a valid attempt nevertheless, to create through sound the totality of time, the ground-bass of duration in human life—present tense being the predominant mode of occurrence, return suggesting past tense imposed on the felt present and future tense as a potential goal towards which everything strives for completion and final resolution. The three dimensions of the human experience of time—past, present, and future—are potentially inherent in the durational process of music perceived as organized sounding pitches. Hence its unfailing power, particularly in Western music where duration as time-span has developed forms which are capable of embodying the durational process in artistically meaningful orders.

I should like now to examine, in the light of the general ideas expressed above, two of the major tendencies prevailing in "advanced" circles today—chance music and total serial music. These two kinds of music define the polar extremities within which composition is now taking place: chance music which operates with situations based on the unpredictability of happenings; and total serial music which purports to operate with situations which are completely predictable. Despite this fundamental difference in approach both operational systems have a great deal in common, and not least a tacit withdrawal from the three-dimensioned durational process already described.

Before going on, I should like first to elucidate one more idea which you may already have inferred from my previous comments. Though the durational process of existence may be uniform for all men in all cultures, it does not follow that existence is viewed in the same way in every epoch. Each culture stresses one or another aspect of its durational experience according to the prevailing philosophical, scientific, or religious modes and beliefs. For a culture in which tradition and conservatism are particularly strong the past undoubtedly has greater importance than the present and future. In such a society the present exists to conserve the past and to transmit its experience to the future. In a society where the ties with history have been loosened or abandoned and the weight of the past thrown off, the present and future suddenly assume the greatest importance because these are the true moments, actual and anticipated, in which life is lived and is to be continued for its own sake.

The predominant philosophical mode of our time is acknowledged to be existentialism, a view of life which holds that the present moment is the nodal point of existence. It is in the present that existence is actual, most vital; before there can be being, there must be existence. One's sense of being derives from one's sense of existence. The way to sense one's existence is to charge each present moment with content and meaning. The present is reality. This view, though distinctly Western in origin, stemming from the thought of Nietzsche, Kierkegaard, Heidegger, Jaspers, and others, finds strong reverberations in Eastern Zen Buddhism, which also holds that the present moment is supreme reality.

It is not at all strange, therefore, that composers of chance music, particularly, are drawn to Zen and imply in their attitude towards music an existential tendency; that is, see music as the occurrence of unpredictable events, each moment of sound or silence freed of formal connection with the moment before or after, audible only as a present sensation, an ensemble of musical happenings of undetermined form or length. The same work may be as long or as short as the performance situation requires. Nothing, theoretically speaking, is known in advance of its occurrence except the frame within which sounds are to occur. The performance is the realization. In this form of existential music, the present erases the past by allowing no recall or return; and promises no future since the present happening is sufficient to itself, requiring no future event for its understanding. This music (or ensemble of sounds and silences) is ever-present to itself at each instant of its occurrence (we cannot speak of an unfolding here). Because this is so, no contextual preparation is required for any event; but just for this reason there can be no surprise because everything is surprise. Duration in the sense of a process incorporating a human past, present, and future in its stream of movement is no longer possible in this music. It is confined to the sound sensation of the moment, leaving no visible trace behind. As music it is like the individual who lives without a personal history, without a sense of his past or hope of the future and therefore with no sense of the continuity of his unique identity. All he knows are immediate sensations; their nature or order of sequence have no meaning for him beyond their immediate pleasure or pain. The proponents of chance music relegate history and tradition to the realm of meaninglessness. The sound of this music is to have no associations with anything tainted by history and tradition; it is to be self-sufficient, unique in its occurrence, divorced from the human situation because it is "free" of cultural contingency. Chance music is the epitome of the unpredictable itself, like life. Caged within the present moment, chance music cannot articulate the totality of duration, only the existential point from which the totality could stretch back and forth but in this case refuses to do so. This declared descent into irrationality erases any possibility of the creation of forms which in their durational aspects can engage the listener's innate sense of duration. All the listener can hope to do is grasp at each occurrence, just as he grasps at life's formless succession of events, hoping to derive some meaningful order. In the case of chance music this is hardly likely; and, from the point of view of the composers of such music, highly undesirable. Thus duration, in the sense we have described it, cannot be said to exist in this music since it is contradictory to its fundamental premise. The anti-order of chance music has no need for memory and its powers of recall; therefore it deprives the listener of his most powerful affective and mental apparatus for seeking order in himself and his experiences, including that of listening to music. Chance music would reduce its listeners to creatures subsisting wholly on stimuli-response situations; creatures who bring nothing to the moment of stimulus and take nothing away from it. Culture and its transmission are no longer possible under these conditions. It makes one wonder whether chance composers recognize the extent to which they have stripped themselves of the hard-won human characteristic of being able to transcend mere sensation in order to form it in ways that communicate to other human beings the transcendent quality of human experience.

When we consider duration in relation to total serialism, we are faced with a completely different set of problems because, while chance music operates with wholly irrational situations, total serialism is supra-rational, that is, it applies to all aspects of musical composition a controlled programme of action based on predetermined relationships derived from number and mathematics. In such a programme the irrational is theoretically inadmissible. However inadmissible it may be to its practitioners, I have tried to show recently in a discussion of "indeterminacy in the new music" that, practically speaking, irrationality is ultimately the victor. But my main concern here is duration as we find it in the music composed according to the programme of total serialism.

Duration is one of the so-called parameters upon which a composer, using serial devices, can project a pre-arranged order. This order of occurrence of durational lengths is organized according to the particular and specific rationalization required for carrying out these operations in relation to the parameters of pitch, dynamic, timbre, and register. It is significant to observe that these other parameters belong to the realm of musical space. Total serialism thus accords an equivalent status to musical time and musical space, the necessary assumption being that duration as musical time must be equally susceptible to precise ordering as are the elements of musical space; otherwise rational control over the compositional situation is lost. The consequences of this assumption are many. I shall mention only those I consider the most pertinent to this discussion.

First of all, duration is no longer a process. Duration now becomes objectified in series of concretized segments or lengths of either clock-time, as in electronic music, or metronomic time as in serial instrumental music. The durational process as such is cast aside in favour of controlled lengths of microcosmic time, which are considered as discrete elements as are pitches, dynamics, and so on. We have known all along that pitches are discrete, specific, identifiable entities. But until total serialism, duration has never been characterized as a series of discrete, specific, identifiable segments of time. True, musicians have always concerned themselves with rhythmic and metrical problems and the conventions of our notation have built up a system of the smallest to the largest possible notational lengths. However, these lengths were never intended as objective, discrete elements but rather as symbols created for the purpose of guiding in a meaningful way the flow of musical time; in short, to make possible the notation of musical time and therefore its performance. Second, duration in music and pitch stem from two different sources, making their equivalence status in total serialism thoroughly arbitrary and suspect. Pitch, as a discrete element comprising measurable vibrations of a sounding body, is external to man even though man is able to produce it vocally. Pitch exists in the phenomenal world as determinate or indeterminate musical sound or noise, depending on whether it is regular or irregular in its vibration. Even though man may produce it in his inner ear as internal, imagined sound, the fact remains that his greatest joy is in producing it physically as actual sound. For man, duration on the other hand is an internalized process, its passage noted by discrete events occurring externally, but in itself an unmeasurable flow insusceptible to limits or demarcation except as in music in the symbolic use of notated time lengths or in life by the general terms with which we refer to the durational process—past, present, and future, terms provided us by language. To equate a non-discrete durational process with discrete pitch elements is to lack all understanding of their separate natures. Third, pitch is material and therefore susceptible to objectivization and rational discipline. Duration is non-material; it can only be felt. To objectify duration in the rationalized, arbitrary fashion of total serialism is to deprive it of its dynamic power to accumulate itself in motion and movement and culminate in a perceptible form. Finally, in serial music in which duration is equated with musical space and its constituents, durational proportions (or time lengths) are co-extensive with spatial proportions. They share equally in the sound-structures of which they form the integral parts. Sounds thus ordered, though occurring in succession, do not necessarily produce direction. Duration, whose natural tendency is to create a sense of direction in time (and therefore in form), thus becomes antidynamic and loses its form-giving properties. The articulation of time as process, not of durational segments, is what creates form. If total serialism thus deprives itself of the natural power of the temporal process to create direction and form, in what then does the form of total serial music subsist? Essentially in the carrying out of the pre-rationalized programme. When all the possibilities of a rational plan of action have been carried out, the composition is completed. Time is spanned, not as an organic process in which a form becomes perceptible growth, but in the same way a clock ticks off seconds, minutes, and hours, mechanically marking measured distances with structured sound events but never realizing time as a dimension of human experience.

Serialism of this type is, therefore (like chance music, but for different reasons), another kind of "existential" music. Antidynamic, its structures exist in the moment they are sounding. Perceptually, it is bounded by each moment. By equating duration with space the former is robbed of its dynamic, autonomous energy. Duration takes on the qualities of the spatial constituents of music: it becomes static, arrested, incapable of directed flow. The supra-rationalism of total serial music defeats the durational process in the end; that is to say, it does not engage the listener in his most profound intuitive relation to life and experience, through his grasp of duration by means of which he creates and recreates the order of his personal identity and therein finds his being.

Ernst Krenek (USA)

Two years ago I caused some raised eyebrows when, in a lecture, I stated that in turning to serialism the composer has liberated himself from the dictatorship of inspiration. People who almost religiously believe inspiration to be the only legitimate source of artistic creation did not like to hear this. What I meant was that in serial music the progress of the work does not depend so much on what comes into the composer's mind at any given moment, but on what is demanded by precise advance planning. Of course, the traditional composer too worked according to some plans, but while the purpose of such plans was the development of structures that were praised for being musically logical, the present planning aims at a structural organization whose coherence derives from the relationships established in a basic order of magnitudes, which order is known as "the series."

The difference may be focussed even more sharply. What in traditional music is described as its inherent logic is its analogy to language and the manifestations of the principle of causality governing speech. Like language, this music formulates ideas, that is, themes that become subjects of progressive variation and development, just as linguistic statements are exposed to varying interpretation in a course of discussion, until a final state of affairs is reached that in some way or other is felt to be the necessary result of the preceding processes. In this respect older music is identified with the concept of non-reversibility, which usually is regarded as an essential property of time.

Traditional music runs in the same direction as time does, but it also sets itself off from time by creating its own metric configurations that seem to float on the stream of real time. The manifestation of this peculiar musical time is the tempo of music. The tempo is defined by how much or how little real time elapses between the pulses of music, that is, between its accented beats. In this way music creates the illusion that it might be able to influence the course of time by accelerating or retarding it. This concept of tempo, materialized in more or less regular alternation of accented and unaccented beats, has become so ingrained in us that music in which this concept recedes into the background or is totally absent appears to resist our perception. To a great extent this is the case with mediaeval religious music. If we are to believe the monks of Solesmes that the individual tones of the plainchant were, as a matter of principle, of equal length, this condition alone certainly did not promote the emergence of the modern concept of tempo. But even when with the ascent of polyphony the acceptance of the rhythmic *modi* of poetry established a discriminatory measurement of long and short elements, the tempo of the music seems to have been regarded as an immutable constant. Deviations from the standard speed were expressed in terms of proportions, that is, prescriptions stating how many notes of a certain category under the new speed would take up the time needed for a different number of notes of the same category under the old speed. It is well known that this manner of thinking led to hair-raising complications, which are by no means less alarming than some of the exploits of present serialism. In fact, it is not difficult to show that some of these modern complexities may well be traced to similar psychological sources, that is, to a propensity for conceiving processes simultaneously moving on at different speeds.

The notion that music has one direction is expressed in the tenets of the system of functional harmony. We remember how our harmony exercises were scrutinized by the schoolmasters for "wrong progressions." The term "progression" as such indicates the concept of music's moving in one direction, from point to point, from beginning to end. Correct progressions were "logical," wrong progressions produced nonsense, just as in speech. When atonality replaced functional harmony by the much less definite, much more flexible principle of controlling the degrees of tension existing between simultaneously sounding tones, the one-way progress of music became less convincing. The twelve-tone technique has reintroduced to musical thinking the notion of the retrograde form, with implications at first perhaps not fully appreciated—a notion that had been practically dormant since the late Gothic polyphony. Even so, Schoenberg used the retrograde forms of the row mainly as a welcome addition to, and variation of, the roster of basic sets. Only Webern began to create truly reversible models that may be, and are being, played in either direction.

Some years ago an atrocity story was passed around to the effect that somewhere a nasty person had taken the trouble of recording some atonal composition backwards, and how he put the experts to shame when he played the record for them and they did not notice

1. Gunther Schuller (USA): "Composer and Performer"; "Some Other Paths"
2. Alfred Frankenstein (USA): "Composer and Public: *The Critic's Role*"
3. Henri Dutilleux (FRANCE): "Some Other Paths: *Diversities in Contemporary French Music*"

6. Karl-Birger Blomdahl (SWEDEN): "Opera and Ballet"

4. Panel: "Synthetic Means": Josef Tal (ISRAEL); Hugh LeCaine (CANADA); Edgard Varèse (USA); Otto Luening (USA); Vladimir Ussachevsky (USA); Lucianio Berio (ITALY)

5. Panel: "Serialism": Iain Hamilton (GREAT BRITAIN); John Weinzweig (CANADA); George Rochberg (USA)

7. Vassily Kukharski (USSR): "Composer and Public"

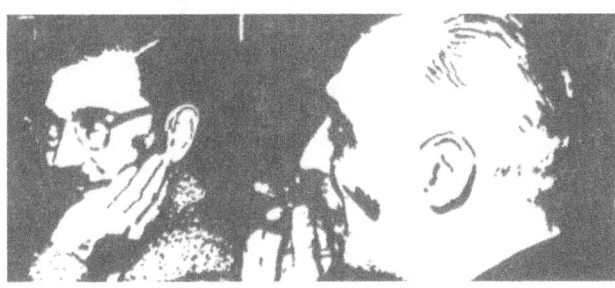

8. Ernst Krenek (USA) and Aurelio de la Vega (CUBA) talk with Jean Papineau-Couture (CANADA) and Constantin Regamy (SWITZERLAND)

9. Conference Concert: A rehearsal of Edgard Varèse's *Deserts* for winds percussion and magnetic tapes, performed by the National Festival Orchestra and Wind Ensemble. The conductor was Frederick Prausnitz; the composer watched from the wings; the bank of percussion and the other "instruments" gave a special look to the platform.

The illustrations are abstractions from photographs originally taken by John Max (2, 3, 9), Peter Smith of Stratford, Ontario (1, 4, 5, 7), and the *London Free Press* (6)

the trick, but praised the wonderful new piece. The villain, of course, wanted to prove that this music did not make any sense even when played in the direction planned by the composer, if one could turn it around without noticing any difference. In the light of recent developments the experts would not have to blush. Just as it is obviously possible to appreciate an abstract painting from whichever angle one looks at it because the notions "right," "left," "top," and "bottom" are not any longer inherent in the object, we can visualize music in which the notions "earlier," "later," "forward," and "backward" have become similarly relative—and irrelevant.

Consciousness of the direction of music is further corroded by the atomization of time that is a consequence of subjecting the element of time to measurements derived from the basic order of magnitudes, that is, to serial organization. If the durations of tones and sounds are determined by serial definition instead of resulting from the impulses of inspiration conditioned by psychological or traditional factors, by association, description, illustration, symbolism, and such, the measurements thus arrived at will not only be, so to speak, abstract, but also of high complexity. Consequently the notion of tempo as a perceptible measure of pace will not be applicable to this type of music. Here again the demand for new modes of perception arises from the very nature of serial music.

A great variety of operations is available for the predetermination of time values. So far the basic order of magnitudes, that is, the series to be regarded as the fountainhead of the entire construction, has been usually derived from certain measurable aspects of the tone row, such tone row usually containing twelve tones as long as the music under consideration is meant to be performed on traditional instruments, or any chosen number of pitches whenever electronic sound production is contemplated. Deriving the necessary sets of magnitudes from certain aspects of tone rows is desirable as long as one accepts as the primary and indispensable motivation of serialism—so to speak, its ethics—the idea that all phenomena of the work ought to be traceable to one unique perceivable source. This, however, is not a necessary assumption. It is possible to visualize a totally abstract numerical series which will not only determine all other aspects of the music, but also the selection of pitches, or the tone row to be used.

If we start with the tone row, as has usually been done so far, its most obvious measurable quantities are the intervals formed by the successive pitches. Two methods of measuring them are available, as is well known: the sizes of the intervals may be expressed in terms of fractions that represent the ratios of the cycles, or they may be expressed in terms of some linear unit, such as half-tones, sixth-tones, thirteenth-tones, cents, or any other such unit of measurement. It seems to me neither necessary to investigate which of the two methods sticks closer to the nature of the musical material, nor convincing to claim that one of them does, as has been maintained by a few serial composers. I have always felt that, whatever the so-called natural sources of music may have been, it has travelled a long way to reach a status in which the behaviour of its particles cannot any longer be referred to alleged primordial conditions.

To some of the serialists who are inclined to believe that their inventions are so startling as to usher in a new era without precedent, it may come as a surprise that the idea of using ratios of intervals for determining time relationships is clearly expressed by Johannes Tinctoris in his *Proportionale Musices* about 1475, as may be seen in the excellent new translation by Albert Seay in the *Journal of Music Theory*. Discussing the proportions *dupla*, *sesquialtera*, *sesquitertia*, and *sesquioctava*, which involve time relationships of 2:1, 3:2, 4:3, and 9:8 respectively, Tinctoris points out that Pythagoras by striking together two hammers whose weights were analogously proportionate produced the corresponding intervals of octave, fifth, fourth, and whole-tone. It is amusing to speculate what might have happened if somebody had constructed hammers of weights corresponding to the more outlandish time proportions of Tinctoris' manual. The result, of course, would have been some very peculiar intervals, and music might well have skipped a few centuries, for better or worse.

Be that as it may, the application of interval ratios to time relations is an arbitrary process. It is true that vibration ratios are a function of time because the intervals between pitches are caused by the differences of the speeds of vibration. However, when the fractions so obtained are used to determine relationships of time spans, their original character is lost, and the resulting measurements are not closer to the true nature of the sounding material than if one had derived them from any other series of magnitudes. As a matter of fact, the serial way of thinking demands by definition a permanent transfer of orderings from the sector wherein they originated to other sectors in which they are not at home. Visualizing this principle from a different angle, I have often discussed it under the heading "rotation," because it involves a serially determined continuous switching of the terms of the series within the compass of the series itself. The process is necessary in order to protect the music from getting petrified in its own tracks because of interminable recurrence of identical situations.

Inasmuch as the numerical values established in the basic series detach themselves from the objects whose magnitudes they originally measured, as for instance the magnitudes of intervals, they become abstract operators. And inasmuch as they impose the ordering of one set of elements on to differently ordered sets, they introduce the factor of randomness into the area of serial operation. For the results of such procedures are by definition random results. For instance, if we took a list of persons alphabetically ordered according to their names and reshuffled it according to the alphabetical order of the streets on which they live, the new sequence of names would have to be called a random result, since it is in no ways deducible from the original sequence, although the basic series is the same in both cases, namely the alphabet.

On the basis of this consideration we can now evaluate the function that is assigned in serial music to the elements of predictability, surprise, and chance. The concept of surprise, which is supposed to be an indispensable ingredient of artistic creation, is obviously predicated upon the existence of standards, an unexpected deviation from which will be experienced as a shock. In traditional music the surprise is engineered by the composer, who knows the standards and decides where he wishes to deviate from them. Consequently he can predict what is going to happen at any given point of his composition because he makes it happen.

The results of serial operations are technically predictable since the variables and constants that cause them to happen are known. The results are practically unpredictable because the processes set in motion by the serial mechanism are far too complex to be visualized in advance. Thus the surprise element is built in. The unexpected happens by necessity. An operation the result of which cannot be predicted is called a chance operation.

When in traditional music the composer seems to be in full control of what goes on in his music, it is understood that he makes the decisions through which he exercises this control by inspiration. Obviously this notion includes a very substantial element of chance since inspiration is defined as the mysterious source that spontaneously produces ideas without the aid of conscious intellectual effort. It is clear, however, that this source does not spring from an absolute vacuum. It is conditioned by the total mental make-up of the individual concerned, his inheritance, environment, habits, training, and countless other influences. Consequently this inspirational source cannot furnish anything that the artist is not able to see with his mind's eye. It is quite understandable and appears entirely legitimate that he might be tempted to operate in areas beyond his own imagination. Ever since this explanation dawned on me, I understood why I had become increasingly tired of the question fired at the creator of unfamiliar music by indignant critics, "But have you really *heard* all the stuff you have written?", as if an answer in the affirmative would produce an extentuating circumstance. The answer should, of course, be: "What does it matter whether *I* have heard what I have written *before* it was written? *You* have heard it *after* it was written, and that should be enough for you to ponder."

Whether the contemporary music that has allowed the element of chance to manifest itself to the extent of letting the nervous reactions of the interpreter influence the ultimate appearance of the composition beyond what these reactions are doing to the music anyway—whether this may still be called serial music is a question I do not feel competent to answer. It certainly is difficult to see how music which is described as indeterminate in its performance can at the same time be determined by serial construction. Perhaps it is not. Its creators are fairly non-committal on the subject, except that I got it two years ago in Darmstadt straight from the horse's mouth that the era of serialism was over. The same horse had explained to me a few years earlier that the era of the twelve-tone technique was over, that in fact such a thing as the twelve-tone technique had never existed. By cool analysis the transition from serial music to chance music could be rationalized by assuming that an originator of musical manifestations who is particularly aware of the presence of randomness in serial music—which I have discussed before—would come to the conclusion that the actual results of serial procedure are not much different from those of chance operation; so that one may save oneself the considerable labour of going into the former. Personally I do not share this view. Not only can one tell the difference, but also I find it more interesting to work with the complexities of a serial scheme than to roll dice or toss coins. But this might be dismissed as a subjective attitude, and we who have done so much to subvert traditional standards should not cast the first stone against anybody by calling his way of doing things an aberration.

From the fact that the latter-day serialists, or post-serialists, devote an extraordinary amount of inventive power to the discovery and unusual application of novel sound qualities, one might infer that they are slightly doubtful about the validity of the musical substance of their creations. On the other hand, the quest for new sounds, in this case undoubtedly stimulated by the experience of electronic sound production, leads to many exciting and welcome innovations. Summing up, I might say that serialism, in order to be practised and understood, demands new attitudes in nearly every sector of musical consciousness. To acquire these one may just as well begin by getting rid of the old ones.

Discussion

Howard Shanet (USA): Talking about "chance music," Mr. Rochberg described it as essentially concerned with the present tense, as compared with the past or the future. Now I know, and I'm sure Mr. Rochberg does, that many composers who don't compose purely chance music use the chance element or the random element purposely to get a new effect, or an interesting combination, thus moving away from any fixed forms. In order not to talk in abstractions myself, let me mention a few names. As early as 1908, Charles Ives, in a very simple little composition called "The Unanswered Question," wrote very clearly fixed lines for several kinds of instruments, but instructed the players not to begin exactly at fixed points with respect to each other, but to take a leeway of several beats in the composition, so that, for example, they could never tell in advance at which moment after the flute had started the strings would come in. There was a random element; but the composer very carefully made the other elements so precise that the formal aspect was perhaps even more marked than in older music. Henry Brant, of Canadian origin but now living in the United States, has done this in a dozen compositions in which he uses the antiphonal effect, so that he has one group of musicians in one corner and three others in other corners of the room; but the individual elements which they are contributing from the other corners of the room are very carefully fixed and have very clearly discernible formal structures—in other words, are not pure cases of chance. I suggest that what we are doing in this analysis is the equivalent of using geometry to describe, let us say, a square or a circle, and then saying that since such and such is a conclusion, it applies to the human face because it is a circle. But the human face is not a circle, and therefore what you say is only partially applicable to the human face, or maybe not applicable at all.

In the same sense, Mr. Krenek talked about traditional musical structures and compared them with language. Of course this is true, but it is not uniquely true nor entirely true. In traditional musical structures you also have analogies to other things—say, to motion. A musical composition of the kind which we are thinking of as traditional has some shapes that have nothing to do with language. They have to do with motion—and I might suggest even with emotion, and I am not using this word in a romantic sense: I mean that just as one has inner disturbances that go with emotion so, let us say, in a Beethoven composition, there are some points which may very well have taken a musical shape from an inner disturbance which is reflected, in parallel or in analogy, in a musical sound that results.

Krenek: I should like to say that I did not deny that traditional music might have analogies to things other than language; I did not deny that at all. I just pointed out this one analogy which to me seems particularly important in this context. But if you speak about emotional qualities in music, I think that these are expressed in a way analogous to the ways of language. These emotions are objects of that expression, if we are so inclined to interpret it that way, but the mode of expression is one which, in some ways, parallels language.

On Mr. Krenek's random remark that he found it paradoxical that a gentleman much younger than himself (referring to Mr. Rochberg) advocates the "middle road" while he himself advocates the extremes, Mr. Rochberg offered the following explanation.

Rochberg: The "middle of the road" is, of course, purely a figure of speech and I don't think it quite accurately describes what I was attempting to say. Instead, I am really concerned with the fact that, if we examine the peculiar cultural situation in which we all exist, we find on all sides a loss of any objective standard by which we can measure anything, and with this loss has also come a lack of tension, which is the same as, let us say, a lack of friction. If we think, for example, of the so-called innovations of a composer like Beethoven, these innovations occur against a standard or in relation to a standard which was the standard of the culture. There were things which were held in common belief. Now when a situation like that faces the creative artist, he then is able to create for himself a personal as well as an artistic and cultural tension. It is out of this particular kind of tension that his art arises, and I think that the whole history of Western culture can be described in a very general sense in terms of this idea of tension. What I am saying today is: let us get back to this tension, let us discover for ourselves something against which we can function as an abrasive because what is happening today is that there is no abrasive. We are floating in a peculiar kind of void and we are at either one extreme or the other. The problem is not the "middle road," which would assume there is no connection between these extremes, but is to take these two extremes and pull them like a rubber band and bring them over here [*gesturing in a circle*] so that this thing is near the breaking-point. Only then will you have the possibility of a new culture, because these are the birth pangs. Unless this happens, there will be no continuation of the genuine culture which is based on existing works, where there is a literature which we can perform, which we can talk about, which we can love or hate and so forth.

Hamilton: I want to mention something which no delegate has yet asked, and which has not come up directly in any of the papers—the matter of the actual direct aural experience. I am not referring to Mr. Krenek or Mr. Rochberg here at all, but sometimes I do hear similar papers read or similar reviews put forward, which are fascinating and go to the very core of things. But when I listen to the actual music or the scores concerned, I sometimes am disappointed to see that the theorizing and the almost physiological thinking about musical problems hasn't necessarily brought about any great originality or new attitude towards the actual sound of the music itself. It happens very often that I read an article in a magazine like *Die Reihe*, and then listen to the music and find that I am faced with exactly the same sound combination that I have heard many, many times before, or with something which is not very much altered from a great deal we have already heard in Berg or Webern.

Otar Taktakishvili (USSR): In listening to this discussion on serial music, I have the impression that we are dealing with only dry computations and calculations and figures. We all know that under the influence of these so-called admirers of "chance music," Beethoven wrote his unsuccessful works [*sic*]. But we don't want to employ mathematical concepts and mathematical instruments in competing with the classicists. When you discuss serial music at great length, you are inclined to overlook the true vocation of music, its task of influencing and acting on human sentiments, human emotions, and the human soul. And in the last analysis the listeners do not experience these great human sensations and emotions in listening to productions of serial music. In this discussion of serial music, my colleague and I have not found any specific or lengthy reference concerning the progress of human thinking and the progress of human sentiment.

Rochberg: What the Russian delegate has just remarked is very interesting because it expresses very naturally a basic point of view which contradicts, I think, the basic premises from which we are discussing this problem. One thing comes through immediately, and that is, that from the Soviet point of view, the musician is an educator of the public. I would like to say, and I believe that my colleagues in the West would agree, that it is a sufficient task to write good music and perhaps from time to time to appear on a panel like this and discuss our mutual problems, without the necessity of also taking upon ourselves the problem of educating our society. Education is also an *indirect* process and if we create good works (and we all hope that we will have this good fortune) then society will be the benefactor. But, as I say, this is an indirect process and we should not as musicians be concerned, except if we are pedagogues in a university or college, with the problem of educating the public.

I would also like to refer to the first remark made. I would like to ask as a rhetorical question: What is dry about the problem of duration, which was the subject of my paper?—since it affects human existence and the way in which one responds to experience, the way in which one achieves one's sense of being and identity through a reflection upon past experiences and anticipation of one's future existence. To me this seems to be right at the core of being alive and being human, regardless of where or under which government one exists on this planet. We are not competing with the classicists; we live under an entirely different kind of cultural system; we have different problems from those which faced Beethoven—and so our problems must be our own. Therefore, in solving them there is no question at all in our minds of our attempting to compete with Mozart, Haydn, or Beethoven.

I should like to comment further on the question of "audience reaction." We too are audience participants. Even though we compose music from time to time, we are listeners to other composers' works. While our listening may be slightly more acute than the average layman's, or slightly more biassed from our own personal point of view than the average layman's, we also react to music, and very strongly. But to turn to the layman, we have witnessed in New York for example, in the last two or three years, a remarkable phenomenon and that is the success of *Wozzeck* by Alban Berg at the Metropolitan Opera. Now the audience there was not full of composers, I assure you.

Hamilton: If you perform in London or in Liverpool or in Glasgow the music from Schoenberg onwards, you get an audience as enthusiastic for this as for anything else. You may not get an audience of the same magnitude, but you will get a large audience which is not a specialized one, who will come and listen. Therefore, people are interested if they are once allowed, through concert promoters, to hear the work.

But what I cannot understand about the initial part of the question—and this is an attitude that is not confined to the Soviet Union only—is: Why do many people think that classical composers were so concerned with subjective things and highly emotional things, with their soul the whole time, when their works, as we have them, were so perfectly constructed, so beautifully calculated, and so beautifully written? They were equally concerned, in different ways, with many of the technicalities that concern us today. It is a small section of the romantic thought of the nineteenth century which assesses creative activity in terms of an outflowing and an out-pouring of effusive emotion. This is not, by any means, the attitude of creative minds in the whole of music. Why should the Soviet speaker, and many other people in other countries besides Soviet Russia, think that composers and creative artists should always be concerned purely with this limited attitude, which is after all an unconscious part of anyone who creates anything? You don't have to bring it out into the open and think about nothing else and condemn everything which has nothing to do with it. It would deny any intellectual participation in any creative artist in any time. I'm sure that has never been the case.

SOME OTHER PATHS

Henri Dutilleux (FRANCE). *Diversities in Contemporary French Music*

We hear a good deal about the "malaise" or the "unsettled state" of the arts today, about the "impasse" in which music, in particular, finds itself. I find such pessimism without foundation; yet we are all aware that we are living in a period of transition, characterized essentially by an extraordinary acceleration of scientific advances, advances which clearly exert their influence on the composer—a figure long misrepresented in the guise of a dreamy and romantic poet. The composer wishes to be "of his own time," just as he always did, and there is reason to believe that in 1960 he is adjusting comfortably. Centres of experimental music spring up almost everywhere. At the same time, among the festivals which burgeon at every point of the globe, there is hardly one which does not give over part of its programme to displays of experimental music or discussions on the problems which rise out of these researches. One cannot but approve such enterprises as these, which show how great is the desire for discovery and enlightenment held by composers today.

Far from assembling here to view an imaginary "unsettled state," we affirm on the contrary that our art is in perpetual movement; and if some observers find their feeling of music's being at an "impasse" now untenable, this is perhaps because they based it in the first place upon the relative lack of interest of the public in an important segment of the contemporary repertoire. This criterion, however, cannot be a valid one; history proves that the work of art almost always seems, by its novelty, to partake initially of the esoteric. This is a cross a great many masterpieces have had to bear at their inception: only in 1960 is the public conscience ready to recognize, for instance, the prophetic quality in certain of the discoveries of Edgard Varèse.

Nevertheless, the very richness of our era can present certain dangers. We composers look on, as marvelling spectators, at the birth of a completely transformed sound-universe; we are thrilled by such riches—but we also may well experience a kind of vertigo in noticing how great is the disparity between our technique, acquired by traditional methods, and the new and necessary discipline which the mastery of these fresh elements of expression demands of us. It seems to be a question of an almost total reconversion of our technical upbringing, and this is something which, though we may not realize it, is generally repugnant to our imaginations. There are many among us who do not possess the spirit of a Stockhausen and would find little pleasure in spending months in impressive laboratories such as those of Cologne, or in adapting themselves to that new compositional craft (as proposed by Pierre Schaeffer of Paris) which alone can organize in orthodox fashion the mysterious *objets sonores*. Doubtless we have here a question of age, temperament, and sensibility. Personally, the worthwhile things I have heard, among the electronic and *musique concrète* pieces so far realized, constitute for me a stimulant—but nothing more than that. The music I write would perhaps not be the same, were I unaware of them. They are in some fashion a nourishment for me, on the same level with an *avant-garde* drama, a good example of abstract painting, or a bold and up-to-date piece of modern architecture.

But at the same time I feel towards them a kind of detachment, somewhat as though it were a case of a new dimension. I am well aware that in saying this I render homage involuntarily to the proponents of synthetically composed music: but are we not witnessing nowadays precisely that—the birth of a new dimension, the beginnings of a new art-form which might be to music what, for example, the film is to drama?

Whatever interest there may be in these demonstrations, it would probably be dangerous to regard them as the only events of importance in these past few years from the point of view of the evolution of the language of music. I think a very great freedom should always govern the realm of art; the greatest danger would be to try and establish, once and for all, the limits of the new contemporary language. Such limits could not be sanctified to the service of experimental talents alone, any more than dodecaphonic music—an infinitely stronger pole of attraction—could possibly be considered the only way open to musicians of enterprise.

To me it is an excellent thing that a Jean Françaix has not the same preoccupations as a Boulez. In saying that, I align myself with neither one artist nor the other; indeed I find myself as far from sympathizing with the one's aesthetics as with the other's. Again, to me it is reassuring that musicians as different as Shostakovitch, Copland, and Messiaen should be contemporaries, as are Britten, Dallapiccola, and Frank Martin, to choose an equally assorted trio of names. It would be distressing, I think, if Badings and Stockhausen were suddenly to turn to mutual mimicry on the slender pretext that each in his own country is absorbed in questions of acoustics and electronics.

It is, in my opinion, against the trend towards standardization of the newer expressive tools that we ought to react. This trend is potentially one of the greatest dangers of our era. It could well destroy the ethnic peculiarities of our various countries. Recordings and radio, which are our powerful and irreplaceable allies, might conceivably betray us by supporting such trends, which, as they develop, lead us bit by bit towards a state of musical cosmopolitanism where finally all original art disappears. We must struggle to preserve, in each country, the notion of a "national art." We may recall Jean Cocteau's happy way of putting it: "A poet never sings so well as when he is in his family tree."

But we must at the same time, above all else, treat with suspicion anything smacking of dictatorship or authoritarianism in the realm of aesthetics. Let us remember how short a time it took for a certain Dr. Goebbels to brand a number of artists as practitioners of "degenerate art," and in the same blow to strike from the programmes the names of Schoenberg, Milhaud, Dukas, and even Mendelssohn—a decision which had, however, the effect of strengthening the resolve of other prominent musicians, such as Bartók and Hindemith, who then took by their own choice the road towards freedom.

Certainly freedom is necessary for the existence of art—and this is so to such a degree that one deludes oneself in insisting that composers should assume an eclectic attitude when passing judgment on a music which is not their own. I do not even believe it desirable that all composers assembled here should find too soon a basis of agreement in their discussions. That could lead them all to write the same music in future—not a heartening prospect. Then, too, we would have no pretext for organizing composers' conferences, at Stratford or anywhere else—and that would surely be a pity!

With all these things in mind, I want to speak to you about some composers of France. They do not always agree very well among themselves; they are in fact often separated by harsh controversies; but I have grouped them together for the sake of discussion, simply because their music seems to me characterized by the single worthwhile criterion: authenticity.

Please do not be surprised if I lay no very great stress, in my presentation, on those composers whose music was already much played in the between-wars period, and whose reputations no longer remain to be established. The composers I plan to deal with, whose number I have rather arbitrarily fixed at six, are generally less familiar to you, and are very different from one another in training, styles, and aesthetic preoccupations. But they have something essential in common. In effect, through their works they explode the widely held notion by which French music is held to confine itself to the realms of "charm, elegance, and *esprit*." They long ago put an end to that false tradition, to which some of their elders perhaps may have seemed exaggeratedly attached. They have thus no taste any longer for salon trifles of sickly scent, but they have rediscovered—we see it in the works of Messiaen and Jolivet, as at an earlier date in Milhaud's—the spirit of the broad fresco. They have at last recognized in Berlioz, so long denigrated and misunderstood by his countrymen, one of the most important of French masters. (Henri Barraud, one of our best contemporary composers, has devoted a remarkable book to him.) As for their technical researches, they have stopped limiting these solely to the fields of harmony and counterpoint, and have acknowledged the value of the least fully developed element in Western music, namely rhythm.

I need not recite for you the biography of André Jolivet. His chief works—the piano concerto, the concerto for *ondes Martenot*, the two piano sonatas, the first and second symphonies—are probably known to you. One of his most recent pieces is *Epithalame*, composed for twelve-part "vocal orchestra". I would have you hear his opinion on the problems of the revivification of musical language:

One seeks this revivification, not by a discipline, but rather by an awareness, gradually becoming deeper and truer, of the human being—the universal or cosmic human being. In what I do, I want to feel free to use every sound-resource discovered by my predecessors, as well as others so far hardly exploited. As for the way in which I approach the writing of this or that score, I prefer to say nothing: it would be mere kitchen talk. Least of all would I want to speak of recipes, ingredients, "tricks of the trade." I find there is too much talk of such matters. The result is the only thing that counts.

When we speak of André Jolivet (who, we might note in passing, was a pupil of Varèse, before working with Paul le Flem), it is impossible not to be reminded of Olivier Messiaen, to whom he is related by many ties both of friendship and of aesthetic thought. Among the works of Messiaen, of which the most celebrated have long since been heard the world over (one thinks of the three *Petites Liturgies*, the *Turangalîla Symphony*, the *Ascension*, the *Vingt Regards sur l'Enfant-Jésus*, the *Visions de l'Amen*), there is a very recent one which I feel to be of special importance. This is the *Catalogue d'oiseaux*. Very advanced in its language, very original in its style of piano writing and in its conception of form, this composition seems to me to occupy an exceptional place in contemporary musical literature. Using a single piano, Messiaen expresses himself fully in a work lasting no less than two hours— at that, it is only the first part of a longer work he is planning to complete. That the preoccupations with acoustics which have always haunted Messiaen, and unquestionably to his enrichment, are again strongly evident is all the more remarkable in view of the fact that the composer here has at his command only the piano.

Here is what he himself tells us of his intentions:

Nature, birdsongs—these describe my passion, and also form a refuge for me. For about eighteen years now, I have been transcribing birdsongs. In the days of my first transcriptions, I would often find myself undecided as to the attribution of a certain song or the identification of a bird. Accordingly I sought the assistance of field specialists and became considerably indoctrinated in the course of guided trips. Realizing it would be impossible for one man to learn, and then to pick out, hear, and note down the upwards of 10,000 bird species extended around the world, I resolved to restrict myself to one country, France. I undertook expeditions in certain districts, accompanied by local ornithologists—Camargue, the island of Onessant, Hérault, the Eastern Pyrenees, the Banyuls area. Each spring, armed with pencils, erasers, music manuscript paper, draughting cardboard, and enormous field-glasses, I would survey a different French province, in pursuit of my masters.

This is how I came to write the Catalogue d'oiseaux *for piano solo. The translation of timbres was especially hard, above all in terms of the piano. Everyone knows that timbre is the result of the greater or lesser number of harmonics present in a sound. Thus I had to find unprecedented combinations of sound, to invent anew at every turn and for every bird. On the other hand, the piano, by reason of its extended range and the responsiveness of its attack, I found to be the only instrument capable of vying, in rapidity both of tempo and of pitch-displacement, with those great virtuosos, the birds.*

Messiaen's activity as a teacher is just as intense as the composing side of his life. Having been professor of harmony at the Conservatoire, before assuming its courses in musical analysis, he exerted a tremendous influence on younger composers, among whom it suffices to name the most noteworthy of his pupils—Pierre Boulez, Serge Nigg, Maurice LeRoux, Yvonne Loriod, Jean-Louis Martinet.

Could one ever imagine two personalities more dissimilar, more violently opposed, than those of Nigg and Boulez? Observing the contrast between them is enough to justify a debate on "diversities (should one perhaps say incompatabilities?) in contemporary music." When one knows the music Nigg is now writing, one can scarcely imagine that, after having been a disciple of Messiaen, he was, like Boulez, attracted to dodecaphonism. This lasted, however, for a relatively brief period only, and his subsequent evolution has followed a line diametrically opposite to that of his former class-mate. To be convinced of this, it would be fascinating to hear his recent *Violin Concerto* immediately followed by the *Second Piano Sonata* by Boulez.

But every bit as interesting as comparing their works is to place in opposition written statements of Nigg and Boulez. First let us hear Nigg:

In order to compose after solidly established principles, I aligned myself with dodecaphonism. After the Rite of Spring *there was no longer anything in music to demolish, and in the twelve-note technique I found an elaborated system which seemed to correspond to the ideas I then held of natural evolution in music. I have pleasant memories of those times. My comrades and I felt buoyed up with enthusiasm and sincerity. They were heroic times. Twelve-note music was not in fashion, and from the public's point of view we were going against the grain.*

But Nigg then adds:

I was, for years, the prisoner of conceptions that were artificial, made-up, desiccated, unhealthy.

And he further adds some thoughts as to the impossibility, in his view, of dodecaphonic music's expressing anything other than melancholy, anguish, despair, nervous tension, and so on.

Now let us turn to the words of Boulez:

It goes without saying that such a conception [that of serial music] can only offend the proponents of a now lifeless tradition, since the latter unfortunately tend too much to look on their thinking habits and their routines as unchangeable natural laws. However, systems appear "systematic" (there is no more humane term for it) precisely until such time as the habit of living with them, and by them, lends them this divine aspect. There is no musical system which is absolutely justified in terms of natural law. Would it not be more to the point to look for a sort of law governing the evolution of the various systems themselves? One may roughly define a system as a group of procedures designed to ensure maximum coherence in the handling of sound-phenomena. When it ceases to have a real necessity for existing, it becomes rotten and falls into disuse.

To rid us of our prejudices on the subject of "natural order," to re-evaluate acoustical knowledge in the light of recent experiences, to describe for us the problems posed by electro-acoustics and by the electronic techniques—such is the course which presents itself at this time.

Let us now leave Messrs. Nigg and Boulez to their debate and have a look at what is happening around them. Here we find, most strikingly, a solid little band of composers on whose foreheads the critics and musicologists have stamped for all time the word "independent." Under this heading are often grouped Maurice Ohana, Marius Constant, or Maurice Jarre; Jean Louis Marinet, Jean Martinon, or Marcel Landowski. This classification, while commodious, is all the same a most arbitrary one; if these composers perhaps do share a great desire for independence, they also bear witness in their works that they are able to form choices as to aesthetic principles; they seldom permit themselves to deviate from the lines they have marked out for themselves—contrary to what one may gather from the label "independent," a term one may well tend to understand in a pejorative connotation.

These composers, however, know how to attune their convictions to their writing, as is proved by placing a declaration of Maurice Ohana's alongside a very impressive work of his, which has been made widely known by recordings, at least in Europe: *Llanto por Ignacio Sanchez Mejias*, inspired by a poem by Frederico Garcia Lorca. Here is what Ohana says about the future of music:

I am always surprised by artists' prophecies, and take them far less seriously than their works. How can one predict a gloomy future for music, when everything nowadays tends towards its growth, towards lending it more and more numerous means of expression? In the current confusion of aesthetics and doctrines, one may find reasons for unrest, but there are also some obvious signs that already the instinct, the intuition, of many creative artists have led them to do some basic speculative thinking. The essential thing is that music should convey, along with the other arts, the secret and truthful image of an era.

Intentionally, I resolved to leave to the end of this paper a few remarks about a thirty-five-year-old French composer, Marius Constant, who, as I have already said, is also generally catalogued among the "independents." Among the composers who have come to the fore in the past decade, he is certainly one of the most remarkable, if not the most gifted, of all. The author of several very successful ballet scores, a piano concerto, and a radio work (*Le Joueur de Flûte*) which won him an Italia Prize a few years ago,

Constant seems to show, in each of his scores, that a synthesis of all the expressive means of today is not only possible but desirable. His most significant work is, in my opinion, the symphonic work which he very appropriately calls *Twenty-Four Preludes for Orchestra*, of which Leonard Bernstein directed the first performance in France in November, 1958. Apart from the innovations in the realm of instrumentation with which this score is filled, what attracts me most about it is certainly the novelty of its form.

The concern with the renewal of the larger forms of music, which is felt throughout the world by many musicians, seems to me to be the dominant factor of the past fifteen years. I have taken account of this factor in selecting the works about which you have permitted me to chat with you in detail today. I would never pretend that they represent a sufficiently complete panorama of all tendencies in the contemporary music of France. I aimed only to give you an idea of the "diversities."

Diversities they are; but I see nothing contradictory about them. In any case, they do not disprove the observations which one of our critics, Yves Florenne, published recently in a French journal—observations which concern not just music, but art in general. I find his thoughts so pertinent that I borrow them for my conclusion:

In the present situation of liberation in which, in some way, all art now dangerously exists, every artist must more or less invent a language. The absence of canons, formulas, fixed standards of measurement, universal terms of reference, makes at the same time critical judgment more difficult and illusion (that is to say intellectual or aesthetic charlatanism) easier. One ought to try and discern and denounce these abuses, these often aggressive poseurs, and their dangers; there is something still more serious than being duped or assuming complacency: and that is to refuse to acknowledge new forms of art, even be they (if I may so put it) "informal," revolutionary, and apparently in brutal contradiction to tradition. The important thing is simply this, not to give way to that slightly naïve imperialism by which some of the new forms or formulas would, in and by themselves, constitute the whole of art, present and future.

[*translated from the French by* JOHN BECKWITH]

Zygmunt Mycielski (POLAND)

Is the purpose of this conference a discussion or a trial of the music we call "modern"? When we discuss the composer's craft, we are discussing the historical evolution of musical language. At the Darmstadt and Warsaw festivals of new music, craft is not discussed as much as it has been here. Thus Stratford could become a centre of precise thinking in this regard, if we believe that musical art can be defined before it is created. (Theory usually follows practice. Composers generally do not like to explain their music. However, many composers recently have been discussing their works publicly, even before composing them.)

Where we are most divided is in our analysis of the tendencies, the objectives, and purposes of musical composition. However, our gatherings would have little meaning without this analysis. Here we are, composers in search of music, on this Shakespearean stage like actors in a play of Pirandello. Must the composer discover a music, inside himself, that nonetheless results from his musical environment? Is this spectacle of composers, discussing their own craft, the crises of an ancient art, and its lack of public support, really so pathetic? Let us discuss, among the features now present in our art, its diversity of techniques and its eclecticism.

Some say that the style of a great period is always represented by a restricted choice of elements, ideas, and disciplines. If this were true, the twelve-note technique would be the sign of the flowering of a great new musical art. However, we see now a variety of disciplines, a race to the new, to surprise elements, with often rather dull results. Once the surprise has passed, the work falls into oblivion and becomes dated much more quickly than a phrase of Schubert or Mozart. While we know that nothing ages as quickly as the new— the new at any price—we also realize that a work which has never been new has no chance of survival. I feel that this paradox is only a natural evolution.

Music is a speculative art but only on condition that the speculation be subordinated to an expressive need, that is, to what we have to say. While music may be the expression of a message, it is also an art which is closely bound to its language and to its technical means.

Music oscillates continually between the emotion created by its own technique (as by an acrobat at the circus or by the art of a dancer) and the emotion produced by its phrases, its rhythms, motives, colours. The art of music is a "closed" art, that is, one closely bound to its language. Also "closed" is the art of stained glass which, after flourishing in the twelfth and thirteenth centuries, fell into decadence in the sixteenth. Similarly "closed" is the art of lace-work, reaching its summit in the eighteenth century, and the art of tapestry, of which the summit is probably the famous story of the Unicorn at the Cluny Museum in Paris. This art, seduced by the new multitude of colours, tried, by imitating paintings, to become what it was not, and fell into a decadence which contemporary artists are trying to arrest. Other arts that have shared the same fate are those of the potteries of Limoges and the mosaics of Florence and Palermo.

Of course, Western music with its ten centuries of development is much more universal an art than stained glass or pottery. Our music moved from the monody of plain chant through *organum* and renaissance polyphony to a high point attained by Frescobaldi, Bach, Vivaldi, and Handel. These composers employed consummately and with great liberty a complete polyphony, a wide choice and variety of means, and an even-tempered twelve-note scale which made unlimited modulation possible and revealed the full resources of the orchestra.

However, the even-tempered scale is a violation of the ear. Alain Daniélou explains that this is caused by the suppression of natural beats which produces a fluctuation in intensity: the natural lines of musical thinking are not developed normally. Daniélou justly states that the tempered scale is a musical absurdity, because it replaces the normal ratios between notes (3:4, 5:4, 9:8, 10:8) by other very complex ratios. However, it was only because of this "violation of the ear" that the music of the seventeenth and eighteenth centuries was produced.

In stating that this "closed" art of the seventeenth and eighteenth centuries was based on the "absurd" tempered scale, I am also saying that it contained within itself the germ of its own decay. The masters who enlarged this system of harmony and rhythm searched for purely idiomatic techniques of the voice, violin, or piano, and developed the nineteenth-century orchestra. In reality they were not employing musical means but rather acoustic effects. Beethoven was the first to seek these effects of silence, percussion, interruptions, unnatural dispositions of the chord, unnatural rhythms. (Maybe it was because he was deaf, but in any case he did it.)

The road has been open since Beethoven for the effects of Liszt and Wagner, where even such great masters are guided not only by what they know how to do but also, as a sort of escape route, by what they are unable to do. When, in a mazurka, Chopin writes two or three bars of counterpoint, he always finds a most ingenious way of getting out of it. Why? Because he was technically incapable of finishing it. Wagner uses harmonic richness to make up for his lack of melodic invention. Wagner used enharmonic notes and modulations as a sort of escape route, and Debussy likewise. Stravinsky rediscovered the *ostinato*, which has been so abused since, and the jump of a third in the bass, also as an escape route for what he could not do differently. All the innovations since Beethoven have been escapes for the incompetence of the innovators.

The last great composer to avoid this search for musical extremes was Mozart, who had such a complete craft that he could do anything he wanted without feeling deficient. The high point in expressive means obviously was towards the end of the eighteenth century. This noble art descends with the advent of effects which are abused with all the resources of the symphonic orchestra. Therefore, the decadence does not start with the harmonic exploration of Wagner, Strauss, and Scriabin, but rather at the height of music's glory. Because this art had reached its height a decadence was inevitable—as with any art that is bound closely to its technique.

Pure technique, the virtuosity of the performer in music, is found in dance, sport, or circus acrobats. We should be neither shocked nor worried by this display. This is not being pessimistic. Our Western music is not the only music in existence—and the end of our music is not the twelve-note technique which really started when we began using the even-tempered twelve-note scale. There are many other systems, and painful search will uncover yet more worlds of sound. Our eclectic period of search should be left open to all systems, none of which should terrorize the others by its exclusivism or bore the audience by its monotony or by its choice of means. This is what we feel in Poland, where we are searching intensely in this crossing of tendencies to find some interesting syntheses and solutions which will develop our art, on condition that we be not bound by either side.

Today there exists a special sort of art for festivals and competitions, and for a special public. This art has little meaning for the large public—which nevertheless also needs its artistic nourishment. Artists, specialists, composers, and critics terrorize each other. Some exclude everything that is old or traditional, others exclude all searching for new materials. We in Poland attempt to create art that admits both and is not created only for one critic or for a period of two or three seasons. We will have none of the terrorism of those fanatics who idolize a wholly new art or one that has been dragged up out of the past. If this moment is so difficult for our art, it is because of the enlargement of the world of sound given by the electronic media and *musique concrète*—along with the twelve-note scale which leads to twelve-note serial technique and which reduces acoustics often to a game, an arithmetic game, an acoustic chance in the meeting of sounds. We fall into that which is most contrary to art, that is, instead of making a choice of means, we enrich them so much that the result is grey, dull, boring, and always the same. The richness of language results in poverty of expression. This is because of escapism, escaping that which we do not know how to do, but which composers *did* know before the decadence of our art set in.

Rhythmic irregularities are pushed to fatigue; one form of the row resembles the next one; a noise bores us or makes us laugh because it is imitative of something. A noise always is imitative because it is impossible to create a *noise* that resembles nothing. Art needs order or symmetry of some sort. Our organisms need repetition or variation perceptible by the ear and not just by the eye or by the mind's philosophical inventions. Music is to be heard, although some of us seem to forget or negate this.

What is the purpose of our art? To please the ear, say some; the message that ennobles our soul and our sensitivity, the enrichment of national traditions, the search for universal beauty, the legacy we leave to future generations, or plain *jeu d'esprit*, say others. In any case, all these purposes are realized when the work issues forth from an inner order, a manifold variant of a careful choice.

Our era has chosen nothing in art. It admits everything. There was formerly one rule of our art which was indisputable. One should first imagine, then hear, and then notate as closely as possible what one has heard. However, in our era this principle has been questioned. I feel that in art it is very dangerous to reverse this order, that is, to speculate first, then notate (or manipulate tapes), then hear the finished work for the first time and finally verify what this speculation has given in sound. We find ourselves in an era that seeks its own face and expression, so violated by the development of technique, an era of noise in which concrete sounds envelop us, and loud speakers blare, thus poisoning the silence of nature. The fact that people come to ignore this continual sound is contrary to all notions of musical art, for this art demands constant attention to sound, a collecting of its better elements. I believe that the present research into noise is a result of our present state of affairs. It is better to broadcast *musique concrète* by loud speakers all day long than to broadcast an *Alleluja* of Bach or a quartet of Haydn, for noise demands no concentration. I prefer silence myself; but the world of today needs noise. Music exists only in silence and concentration.

Contemporary music is attempting to escape all effort, to become easy. Today, research in music is really moving towards facility and not, as is commonly believed, towards complexity. It becomes very difficult to produce, but the end result is facile listening. When *musique concrète* becomes well known to the public it will be the simplest thing in the world to understand.

Let us consider the purpose of musical composition, that art in which we imagine a sound first and then hear it, an art that demands concentration instead of exalting our dissipation and need for noise.

In conclusion I quote an extract from an article on harmony by Jean Jacques Rousseau's *Dictionary of Music*. It is a curious foreboding criticism of harmony and counterpoint in the name of the richness and variety of monody.

When I think that of all the peoples of the earth, each of whom has music and singing, Europeans are the only ones who have chords and harmonies and who find this mixture agreeable; that in the centuries of history of all the nations cultivating the fine arts, none have known our harmony, that no birds, no animals, no natural beings create harmony other than the unison, no music other than melody [this is an error]; *that the oriental languages, so sonorous and musical, and Greek ears, so delicate, sensitive, and artistically trained, never guided these passionate and voluptuous peoples towards harmony; that without it their music had such prodigious effects and that with it our music has such feeble ones* [this was written after Bach!]; *that finally it is left to the people of the north, whose hard vulgar organs are more moved by noise than by the soft accents and the melody of inflections, to make this big discovery and to give it as the basic principle of all art; when I think of all this, I suspect without difficulty that all our harmony is an invention of our gothic and barbarous art, and that we would realize this if we were more sensitive to the real beauties of art and to truly natural music.*

[*translated from the French by* BRUCE MATHER]

Constantin Regamey (SWITZERLAND)

Today we are experiencing a radical change not only in musical style but in what we call musical language. It is a change in language as opposed to a change in musical aesthetics such as is to be observed between the Baroque, Rococo, and Romantic movements. In this I agree with the defenders of the *avant-garde* of today. I disagree with them in that I maintain that music must remain a language. By language, I do not mean that music should be capable of expressing precisely a message of human ideas or feelings. Music at the most can only express our reactions, an emotion or attitude to these ideas or feelings, and, although this extra-musical part of the art is very important, its "message" has, over the centuries, varied little, as music cannot enter into detail.

When we say that a composer "has something to say," we mean that he is sincere, spontaneous, and motivated by some force. This is really the "content," the method he uses to express himself, the aural phenomenon with which he creates his musical attitude. If he has extra-musical elements, philosophical attitudes, these have no bearing on whether he expresses himself well or badly in music. We have many composers of genius devoid of any philosophical ideas.

The only truly musical phenomenon is that which can be perceived by the ear. It is very interesting and, for analytic purposes, often necessary, to read articles about certain scores; but their explanations have no bearing on the actual sound that reaches the ear. And by this "sound" I mean the essential sonorities, ideas, and even structures—on condition that they can be recognized by the ear. These recognizable elements in all music are not discussed enough today. Rather, the theoreticians of twelve-note music tell us about the interior *cuisine* of music which can hardly be perceived by the ear because without the explanation of the composer it would take weeks of calculation to find out how the composer ordered his note-series. Therefore, it is impossible to hear this coherence, which is purely abstract and theoretical.

Although music is the only art which has no connection with objective reality, it has nonetheless certain instinctive and direct relationships which are easier to feel than to explain scientifically, such as certain phenomena of tonal music. Therefore it would be a shame to deprive music of these mysterious gifts which give it an instrument of inner coherence apart from those of repetition, of reminiscence—an instrument which seems to be inherent in musical substance. The whole difficulty which embarrasses logical methods is that these relationships, which seem to be part of the natural essence of sounds, change from one culture to another and therefore are not of an eternal metaphysical order but seem to be merely the product of certain eras. This is a crucial question in many theories, in poetics of music, in the creations of "schools of thought" and is a burning issue of our age. Nineteenth-century man believed that the tonal system reflected a certain given but inexplicable truth, although he may have related it to acoustics, to metaphysics, to mysticism, to the symbolism of numbers, to all sorts of things. However, he was bothered by the fact that, while these tonal relationships seemed to be eternally valid, he could not explain their origins. Scientific developments, a better knowledge of music of other centuries and cultures, showed us that something was amiss. I suppose that to the average listener of today understanding Pérotin is as difficult as understanding Schoenberg, although I must suppose that Pérotin was comprehensible to the people of his era.

Similar problems in respect to oriental music are even more acute. We live in the century of universality. We search for the common language everywhere. At UNESCO we have east-west encounters, such as the one in Paris last year which brought such disastrous and shaming results for the occidentals. The oriental musicians all regarded us with mistrust. We realized, with the persuasion of Alain Daniélou, who is more Hindu than French, that our music is considered by them to be pure barbarism in comparison with the great long traditions of India and China. To quote a very fine eastern musician: "Western music is monstrous and of all western music the most monstrous is that of Bach. Bach's music is impure because it is polyphonic; he is false because he uses a tempered scale and because he employs exclusively non-musical elements such as melody, rhythm, and harmony." For an oriental, harmony does not exist, because it is a vulgarity; rhythm and melody are based on given *schemas* which are, to a certain degree, eternal. The work of an artist is what he does with the given *schemas* or patterns, or the little variations and ornaments of their improvised, and thus constantly renewed, music. I saved our dignity a little by saying to a Vietnamese delegate that, if he thought our music was so terrible, what did he think of Indian music? He replied that he thought Indian music was just as hideous as ours. We were only more confused when M. Daniélou explained to us that Vietnamese music is really not very good.

Thus we see that it is possible, in time and in space, to have a diversity of musical values. When we speak of the purpose of the composer to hear the collective voice of his artistic environment, will he discover in this way any eternal musical values? No! These vary between cultures. Consider the different musical reactions of Spain and Norway, of Germany and France, or the typical examples of Bruckner and Fauré. Thus we see that our musical language is a pure convention without historical justification. The main transformations of our language have been from Greek music to Gregorian chant, to the appearance of counterpoint, the appearance of the triad in the fourteenth century which leads to the pan-consonantism of the renaissance, to the seventeenth century, and finally to our transformation which is probably more radical as our means are changing. Of the two schools of thought along these lines the first, the "genetic" school, holds that there are eternal musical laws, be they justified by religious, metaphysical, acoustic, or physiological means, that all changes are a movement towards an eternal totality. Therefore, the purpose of the creator is not to find something new but, like a scientist, to discover something that always existed but was unknown before, that is, a gradual enlargement of our knowledge of an existing reality. (For example, Hindemith even tried to write manuals for music which does not yet exist but which will come later.) The principal failing of this idea is that not only does it not explain many historical developments but also it does not explain today's reality, and thus its foresight into the future is contrived. The second and dominant school of thought is that of the "finalists" who affirm that there are no musical laws except for a few primitive acoustic laws, that nothing else has any justification either in physics or in psychology, that systems which are necessary to create a coherent language are pure conventions, that creators should change their language because of new necessities that appear before them. This is the attitude of the twelve-note theoreticians and it is interesting to see how they explain the history of music and, for instance, the appearance of the leading-note. The weakness of this theory is that when an innovation appears, it is individual and subjective. Why does it become for everyone a powerful force that imposes itself as something natural and spontaneous, and why do we accept certain innovations and reject others?

Both views, I feel, are too extreme, and the truth lies not in the middle but in both. Certain phenomena found constantly in all music relate to acoustics but go beyond that. In every period there is an extension of these laws in excess of their justification and these "illegal" extensions either remain with us or they disappear. For example, in the middle ages, we felt consonance only at the fifth and octave, the third being dissonant; but we find in this period superpositions of fifths to form a ninth (F-C-G ascending), that is, two consonances making a ninth—which was considered more consonant than a triad. This innovation disappeared in the fourteenth century, which moved in another direction. On the other hand, the "illicit" innovation of the third was accepted and maintained up to our time. Thus, there exists an eternal play between certain intuitive given ideas which agree with acoustic and psychological laws, and inventions that are accepted or rejected according to their influence.

It follows that a musical language is obligatory, and, at the same time, arbitrary. As a linguist I can tell you this: languages too are arbitrary, because a word does not need to have one meaning or another, as seen by the fact that there are many changing languages; but for a given group and a given time they are also obligatory, because they must be understood by everyone. A totally personal language would be an impossibility, because it could not communicate. However, each individual ignores this fact to a certain extent and, as a result, languages change progressively. If these individual innovations become comprehensible for other people, it is because slow changes of one innovation at a time become understandable by means of their context. In learning a foreign language we come to understand the untranslatable words by means of their context, not by means of a dictionary. Thus, the desire of our era to break completely the bonds with the past is an error. We are told that to write modern music we have to lose our old habits completely and to create new ones. I wonder how we must create these new methods and on what basis? Naturally, on reading prose commentaries by the *avant-garde* we never develop new aural sensitivity, as this can only be done by listening. In listening to these new works we have to refer to something in our previous experience of musical language—even though we are told that this is the wrong way to listen to them. However, the majority of people do listen in this manner. One cannot suddenly abandon life-long habits of listening. If we hear one day Beethoven and the next day Boulez, we cannot forget today our sensitivity of yesterday. To create something that resembles nothing in the past is not to create something new. A neologism in language is new because it is an old word used in a new way—but when it has no connection with the past it is not a neologism, for it is empty and means nothing.

In French one distinguishes between *langue* (tongue) and *parole* (speech). *Langue* is an ideal, an ensemble of relationships and references that does not exist because no individual of the group knows completely the *langue* and every individual has certain personal variations of it. While *langue* is a collective method of expression, *parole* is what one does with it. In poetry it is a strong effect to go against the language, to modify it, but always in reference to the language. Certain procedures now found in the twelve-note technique were used in the middle ages. At that time, these procedures, retrogrades, isorhythms, and so on, were part of the *parole*, and they had their *langue*, the modes and complex polyphony. Thus these procedures were quite understandable; whereas in twelve-note music one makes of these procedures not the *elaboration* of the *langue* but the *basis* of this elaboration. This is a vicious circle because one wants the language of the work to be a result of the procedures that one applies to this non-existing language. The difficulty is that these works exist; there are many masterworks among them; and when one writes twelve-note music with sensitivity, this sensitivity refers to something other than the non-existing language of the twelve-note technique.

I am often quite struck by violent partisans of twelve-note music, who in analysing a score point out that, "Here the row manipulation is not strict." This means that the composer is not just a simple calculator but also a sensitive artist. To what is he sensitive if the only real basis of this sensitivity should be, idealistically, the structure of twelve-note language? There is another order of reference which I believe is not a tonal one nor based on the calculations of the twelve-note technique. The fact that we cannot explain this order of reference now should not bother us. No valid system in music was ever explained before it existed. It would be no longer valid when explained and codified because art is by its very nature a perpetual evolution.

I don't want to propose anything other than the twelve-note technique because what I criticize in it is a premature codifying and an unnatural development. I have nothing against twelve-note writing—I use it, and write pointillistic music myself—but I am against any theory which finds unessential that which is essential to music. This system produces structures that are very interesting, and also new sounds; but it does not explain the musical phenomenon. Stockhausen once said that no one can see inside the atom but the atom's interior determines its character. However I maintain that in art it is the character of the atom and not what is inside which interests us. The marvel of artistic language as opposed to normal language is that while normal language tries to be precise an artistic work can be seen by different groups or eras in different ways. However, it is always grasped directly by the ear without any need to know its *cuisine* or inner construction.

The reason for not writing tonal music is not that the tonal system is dead. Rather, we cannot write today really creative tonal works because tonal writing would lead to a reproduction of already-existing styles. If we were to write in the style of Mozart, Beethoven, or Brahms, the result would be worthless because it would not be the spontaneous expression of our time or of our psychology. Change is a natural law. If "content" in music is "how" we express certain eternal values, this "how" becomes dull and unevocative after a certain time. We must find other means which will lead to new expression as opposed to new means which communicate nothing.

[*translated from the French by* BRUCE MATHER]

Gunther Schuller (USA)

In casting about for a logical premise by which I might limit our subject, I decided that the best approach would be to talk about those aspects which have interested me and with which I have been actually associated. I thought there would be undoubtedly many discussions and papers on serial technique, its application and its future role, as well as other more radical aspects of present-day music. The subject I shall discuss is much less radical, but may nevertheless have far-reaching consequences.

I should like to make it clear immediately, however, that I do not intend to speak about these matters in a proselytizing manner. I am not interested in the selling of ideas; if my music cannot sell them, certainly my speeches will not. In any case, proselytizing is foreign to the creative spirit. You believe in something and you do it, and that's all there is to it. The effect these ideas might or might not have, and their acceptance, are all basically irrelevant to creative effort. So if I speak about these things, it is only to explain them, to clear up possible misunderstandings.

Perhaps the most unusual aspect of my musical activities has been my espousal of jazz—my attempt to incorporate certain elements found only in jazz into my over-all creative activity. This attitude of mine towards jazz generates all kinds of reactions, from sympathetic approbation and enthusiasm to the raising of eyebrows and outright ridicule. Prototypical of the negative reaction is a remark such as: "Why do you want to bother with such trashy and naïve music? What possible fascination can it have for you as a serial composer?"

Part of the answer, of course, is that jazz is no longer such a trashy and naïve music. The other part of the answer is that jazz, at its best, has a spontaneity and direct communicative power that a great deal of even the best non-jazz music fails to achieve.

It must be abundantly clear by now to open-minded and informed people that the old prejudices regarding jazz simply no longer pertain. Some exceptions notwithstanding, jazz is no longer a red-light-district music played only by dope fiends in smoke-filled night clubs to the eternal accompaniment of clinking glasses. As a matter of historical fact, jazz has moved from the area of purely functional or entertainment music in the direction of becoming a highly specialized, disciplined art form. In the hands of many musicians it has become skilled, expressive, and vital, so that any musician or music-lover with an open mind can listen to it with respect and enjoyment.

I think a great deal of the confusion arises from a misunderstanding of what a composer such as myself means by jazz. Unfortunately too many people—even composers, who perhaps should know better—lump jazz together with rock-and-roll, popular Broadway tunes, and commercial music of every variety. All these parasitic forms are distantly related and bastardized derivations of jazz; moreover they are strictly commercial enterprises that have nothing to do with artistic integrity.

Here the speaker played three recorded excerpts, the first a piece of rock-and-roll, the second a hotel-type dance band, the third a lush commercial arrangement of a popular song, describing them as "not jazz, but a commercial product." These were followed by excerpts from four pieces introduced as samples of genuine jazz: Charlie Parker's improvisation on Lady be Good; *Cecil Taylor's improvisation on Duke Ellington's* Azure; *John Lewis'* Piazza Navona; *and Ornette Coleman's* Free.

Let me make myself quite clear. It is not a question of artistic quality or musical standards, which are always arguable. Rather, it is a question of the avowed intent of the music. My first examples were *admittedly* commercial, synthetic products, while those of the second group—whatever their artistic merits—were sincere attempts at uncompromising musical creation.

You might say: "Even this better kind of jazz is still limited, and its place within the broader context of contemporary music is still a very special and circumscribed one." That may be. But on the other hand, jazz is the most rapidly growing and expanding music in the world. Starting as a crude folk music, it has within the span of only sixty years duplicated and emulated the whole seven hundred years of Western European music, and has now reached a point almost abreast with so-called classical music. In the hands of its most advanced exponents, jazz has definitely reached the more liberated areas of free tonality (or atonality), and is beginning to shake off the tyranny of the 4/4 beat. It is doing these things without giving up its characteristic spontaneity, achieved through improvisation. Improvisation is the life-blood of jazz; it guarantees a built-in human quality; it is not notatable and is therefore largely inaccessible to composers who work only in terms of the written page.

It is significant that a number of prominent young composers, not interested in jazz *per se*, nevertheless show a similar concern for spontaneity and the involvement of the performer in the creative process. I am speaking, of course, of the improvisational and so-called indeterminate aspects of recent works by John Cage, Stockhausen, and others. I don't think that such tendencies, occurring both in jazz and in non-jazz, are the result of mere coincidence. I believe rather that the tremendously increased complexity and the reality of a totally, rigorously organized music have made the investigation of more liberating principles imperative. I think the occasionally frightening prospects and possibilities of total organization were brought home rather forcibly to all of us who attended the recent ISCM Festival in Cologne, Germany. In many instances, the term "New Academicism" would not be entirely misapplied.

It is not my place here to evaluate the extremes of totally organized serial music. The problem is too new, and it could result only in a premature judgment. But I think it is safe to assume that the world of music has room for both directions—technically pure formal order, and its opposite, free and partially indetermined order. It is in that sense that I see certain values and possibilities in jazz. It is after all not such a long way any more from the non-thematic, non-tonal, a-rhythmic, and free-form music that I write to the non-thematic, non-tonal, a-rhythmic, and free-form improvisations of an Ornette Coleman.

We have heard a great deal at this conference about the rhythmic and durational aspects of serial music. And I suppose it is natural for composers involved with the most advanced stages of rhythmic organization to look with some disdain on the apparently simplistic rhythms of jazz, centred as they are on the eternal 4/4 patterns. However, jazz rhythms are really not that naïve. Rhythmic organization has an entirely different fascination in jazz than in contemporary "classical" music. In jazz, with its undeniable rhythmic vitality, the subtleties of rhythm are not based on discontinuity and atomization, but on *continuity* and the attraction of all its rhythmic parts to a central "beat," which pulls at the many rhythmic particles like a magnet. We can think of rhythmic organization in jazz as revolving around a central axis: the beat. And each beat is like a sun with its many satellites circling in a great variety of orbits, yet constantly attracted to the central body. The anticipations and delays with which the jazz musician embellishes the beat are of an infinite variety and subtlety, and are, it seems to me, a natural, spontaneously felt musical phenomenon, which serial composers attempt to achieve (for different reasons) by all sorts of "irrational" rhythms and often unperformable complexities. The rhythms that occur in jazz are not notatable with any degree of accuracy, and any attempt to codify them results in undecipherable notational monstrosities. Their fascination, therefore, lies in their capacity for free expression within a specific order, their complete spontaneity based on creative rather than recreative reflexes, and their capacity for propelling music forward. Jazz rhythms are seldom static or vertically conceived. They are horizontally motivated, and it is this quality that jazz musicians call "swing."

All of this is not to say that the fusion of jazz and/or improvisatory elements with present-day compositional procedures is *the* solution to the problems of contemporary music, or that it is free of serious obstacles. The problems, indeed, are many—both in composing and in performing. Just how these will be solved, only the future can answer. However, there is every indication, as I see it, that these obstacles will be met and overcome.

One of the most common potential dangers is that composers from one side of the musical fence will blithely borrow devices and superficial aspects from the other, or graft one music on to the other. We had our share of that in the 1920's, when a whole genre of hybrid jazz developed. Clearly, the only possible solution is for a composer to immerse himself completely in the intrinsic nature of both musics, and create spontaneously from within these two generative centres. (And here I am not speaking of the appropriation of a folk music by the mainstream of composed music in the sense that Bartók, for example, employed Balkan folk elements. Jazz is no longer just a folk music. It is a highly sophisticated art music with its own set of laws and standards. It is therefore in a position of hearing and contributing equally in any stylistic partnership. Mere appropriation of its nuances is not what I am suggesting.)

Another problem is that there are not yet enough Ornette Colemans. The improvisational styles of ninety-five per cent of jazz musicians are unusable in the context I am speaking of. But then all we really need is the remaining five per cent. I predict with complete assurance that within ten or twenty years the picture will have changed dramatically. The days of the musician who can grow up knowing only jazz or classical music are numbered, as are the days of the jazz musician who does not read music. Once this gap between composer and improvising performer has been closed, I think we can expect a new era in music, where the interaction of inspired improvisation and inspired composition will bring us to the threshold of totally new musical experiences.

For my part, I have tackled this problem from at least two angles, all within the limits of practical considerations. The first approach has been to write compositional frameworks, essentially twelve-tone or serial in concept, with which to challenge the improvising musician into areas he might ordinarily not encounter in his normal jazz practice. This is a dangerous approach (a little akin to walking a tightrope), in which you must always keep the limitations of your improvising player, actual or imaginary, in mind, or else sacrifice the over-all unity of the work. It stands to reason that players versed in more advanced idioms will be able to operate more effectively in such a framework than those whose ear is strictly diatonic.

The second approach—and in this perhaps I *have* been somewhat of a proselytizer—has been to compose works in the jazz idiom for non-jazz performers. This, of course, immediately eliminates improvisation, and implies that everything will be written and notated. Here, the notational problems for the composer are immense, for he must try to blueprint, as it were, the complex subtleties of jazz phrasing. I realize that this second approach is the less important of the two, but I feel that it has a kind of interim place in making orchestral musicians, who are often incredibly hidebound and limited in their musical outlook, aware of jazz as a valid form of contemporary musical expression—as, in fact, a music which is here to stay!

OPERA AND BALLET

Karl-Birger Blomdahl (SWEDEN). *Aniara*

I certainly have no qualifications for talking in general words about opera, having a very limited experience, in fact, having written only one so far: *Aniara*. Moreover I am on the whole very sceptical about generalizations when talking of contemporary art. Each work of art is unique and the motives for creating this work are equally unique. The discrimination of trends and styles and schools and so on is for posterity to do. And for the musicologists. The composer is—as I see it—reliable only when he is talking about his own works. And very often not even then. But he might say relevant and significant things when he talks out of his own experience of actually created works. And such observations, though subjective and limited, might be of more than personal consequence and importance. So—my reflections will be tied to *Aniara*. More exactly, to some aspects of libretto, form, and means, that have been subject to discussions in some articles about opera.

As to the libretto, there is one characteristic it shares with the texts I have used in other vocal works, for instance, the oratorios *In the Hall of Mirrors* and *Anabase*: it is written by a contemporary poet, the Swedish poet Harry Martinson. And this is not mere chance. I do not in any way deny that the essential problems and ideas of man are eternal, more or less the same, irrespective of the era one happens to be born in. But each epoch offers its own variations and finds its own formulations of these essential experiences and problems, and for me, being a composer living *now*, it is not only natural, but necessary to use texts written by poets who share *my* experience of life, the life of our epoch. Only *then* I feel that the essential requirements for a fusion of text and music are there. Personally I would never dream of setting music to a poem by, let us say, Goethe, or a drama by Shakespeare. And if I am attracted to an old text, it has to be so old that it is deprived of every specific mark of period and milieu—that is to say, it has to be a myth.

In the case of *Aniara* it was the grand poetic vision of Martinson's epos, that attracted me: the vision "of our own day and age, of how we ourselves go through life in a spiritual void," "the journey through the destitute and forsaken human soul," symbolized through the journey in outer space many years hence of the spaceship *Aniara*. It should indeed be evident to any listener that his poetic vision also is the central idea of the opera. The frame, the symbols, come from the world of modern science and may have the outlook of "science fiction"; but it was never my intention to try to create some kind of sensational "space-opera." The essence of the opera—as well as of the original epos—is the tragedy of modern man: the disintegration of the spirit in a world of technique where man is the victim of the enormous elemental forces he himself has called forth.

Martinson's epos has a sub-title: A Revue of Mankind in Space and Time. The word revue is very significant already for the form of the original epos and even more so for the opera. Erik Lindegren, the librettist, and I have consciously kept hold of this idea of a revue, as the best solution of a scenic-musical form for the visions presented in *Aniara*. But could not such a conception of form offer new possibilities to opera on a more general level? Is a plot or tale with a clearly cut external course of events the only possible basis for operatic form? The irrationality of opera as such should, I think, in fact indicate the opposite: imaginative, subtle, and complex continuity that has very little to do with plot or narrative, but much more with poetry. Tension, drama, action could be built up by handling musical images similarly to the way the poets use poetic imagery nowadays, when they attain potentiality through the compression of metaphorical language, suppressing "links in the chain" of explanatory and connecting matter, through the combining of contrasting images, through the unexpected clash, short-circuit between metaphors, and so on. Such a procedure modified and adapted to the different components of opera, applied especially on macro- but also on microform, is what I am thinking of, when talking about "revue" in this connection. Not a series of illustrating *tableaux vivants*, but a compressed, dynamic sequence of contrasting scenic-musical images, the pattern of which communicates the essence of the work. Such a procedure could be used for a *buffo* as well as for an *opera seria*.

The word "revue" also suggests another aspect of opera, which I think still is relevant—that of entertainment. Like the popular revue, though on a higher level, it could offer rich opportunity and great variety in using the means of the theatre, in this case the big apparatus of grand opera, and it could give room for new combinations of literature, dance, plastic arts, and music.

When it comes to the question of my view on the musical means I have used in *Aniara*, I first should tell you that my basic idea is that opera is *vocal music* in scenic-dramatic form, that the dominating means of expression are *voices*, tones, sounds, rhythms. Without deprecating the great importance of the other components, it is the quality of the music that ultimately decides the value of an opera. My second idea is a logical consequence of the first: as regards the "message" of the music (and I do believe that music should have something to communicate to the listener, must "get across the footlights"), the musical means must be chosen to that end. As grand opera makes use of a big, very complicated apparatus, and always is performed in big theatres, any kind of intimacy is practically excluded. Structural and expressive subtleties one can effectively use in chamber music or even in an orchestral piece for the concert hall are bound to drown in the monumental sweep of grand opera. Accordingly I think that structural simplicity and transparency are of great importance. But to avoid misunderstanding I should like to point out that the requirements of structural "simplicity" do not rule out a rigorous approach towards the design and use of musical materials, which, to my mind, should be natural to every composer in our day and age.

Another point of view which I think relevant, though it may seem superficial, is that grand opera inevitably must address itself to a broad public and cannot be an exclusive affair to the same extent as other forms of music. There must be reasonable proportions between the big and costly apparatus and the size of the public that can appreciate its products. In the case of *Aniara* these general points of view coincided with a special personal aspect to the problems of the fusion of text and music. *Aniara* represents an attempt to widen my register of expression to meet Martinson's epic style, which in a certain sense is "artless," demanding, as it does, a different type of musical treatment than that to which I have been accustomed when in earlier works using texts of a more "exclusive," complicated nature. In fact the lines of direction I have mentioned—the universality of the subject, Martinson's "artless" epic style, and my general view on means and aims of opera—could with fairly good reason be summarized in the statement that *Aniara* is a conscious attempt to write a "popular opera."

Concerning means, I should like to add a few more specific comments. The music of *Aniara* includes some sequences of "taped" music, partly "concrete" and partly "electronic." My view of the usefulness of the means of expression this kind of music offers is pretty sceptical. As I see it, the electronic means are still in such a primitive stage of development that they cannot be successfully used independently for pure musical purposes. Compared with the conventional instrumentarium, their fundamental expressive power is as yet very poor and insufficient. In *Aniara* the taped music has primarily a specific *symbolic function* in a greater context. And in this limited function, as one component in the field of tension between technique and spirit, space and earth, in this opera, I think these means are adequately applied. But I certainly do not want to have this taped music detached from its context and played separately, because then it loses its essential function and *raison d'être*.

I should like to end with a few words about another special problem of musical means involved in *Aniara*, that of parody. Obviously parody is part of the greater category of allusion. And allusion—as I see it—is very specific expression for an attitude to tradition, a way to actualize and establish a palpable contact with it. In contemporary literature allusion plays an important role both in poetry and prose, and—though not to the same extent—it has also been used in music, earlier as well as in our own day. Parody naturally implies a negative attitude, and in the case of *Aniara* the use of it in both text and music is a natural and logical consequence of the drama itself: the tragedy of disintegration. But there is always a risk involved in the use of parody. The purpose of the negative attitude might not be apparent enough; the ambiguity of allusion might cause great confusion. And something that is meant as a weapon used "for the warriors' permissible purpose of killing and wounding" might be interpreted as—mere eclecticism.

Henk Badings (NETHERLANDS). *Experiences with Electronic Ballet Music*

It seems obvious that electronic music and modern ballet should form favourable combinations. The fact that electronic music attracts both choreographer and dancer is undeniable. This fact is so remarkable that I will try to investigate the possible reasons for it and to report experience so far gained.

In my opinion, the most important peculiarities which distinguish electronic ballet music from traditional ballet music are the following:

1. The tempo of electronic ballet music is constant (apart from small deviations caused by the use of different types of magnetophones); the tempo of traditional ballet music is variable, determined as it is by the conductor's will. Dancers have told me that they appreciate the advantages of the constant tempo during rehearsals and performances more than the loss of a conductor even though he will, by following their tempo variations, avoid possible mistakes.

2. The rhythmic possibilities of electronic music supply us with an arsenal of successive or simultaneous time values of any duration and in any, even irrational, proportion. A measure with beats of unequal length is just as simple as a measure with equal beats in electronic music; a combination of rhythms in irrational proportions is, perhaps, even easier to realize in electronic music than a combination of exactly coinciding, regular rhythms. What the choreographer will consider as "new" in the rhythmic pattern of electronic music will, doubtless, be the hovering effect in combinations of more than two non-coinciding rhythms and the rhythmic effect of a measure with unequal time units. The former inspires a variety of solutions—for instance, the hovering dance motion or the combination of different tempi and different motions for the dancers. The latter does not seem to be problematic as long as it offers the dancer a cadence, a "swing," in the order of beats. I have seen curious examples of dancers performing unequal steps coinciding with this music which they said they had no difficulty in counting.

3. Electronic music has many new tone shapes or tone envelopes at its disposal. These tones that appear mysteriously, without a perceptible attack, captivate the dancer and inspire a weightless, plastic gesture.

4. Usually with electronic music, there is no music sheet at the disposal of the choreographer and, even if a notation exists, it cannot be read or used in the normal way. Therefore, the choreography and the practising must be based on the audible sound. This fact, I believe, influences the results.

5. The sound world of electronic music is new to dancers and it is a notorious fact that unknown sounds have an exciting effect, the so-called "magic" effect. An amusing example of this "magic" effect is the story of the first demonstration of an organ in the cathedral of Aix-la-Chapelle in the time of Charlemagne. Though this organ could hardly have been more impressive than one stop of our harmless harmonium, the effect, in those days, must have been exciting, as it caused many of the attending people to faint. I cannot boast of the same effect being caused by electronic music. But it seems that this "magic" power of the unknown electronic sounds does inspire the choreographer.

6. Another result of unknown sound is that it rouses in the average listener the most extravagant associations. If, after hearing a symphony of Mozart, a concert-goer associated it with a "growling of demons" or with the "harmony of the spheres," we would be inclined to consider him very impressionable if not over-excitable. The utterance of the same or often more exaggerated associations after hearing an electronic piece of music is, however, accepted as quite normal. Even colleagues often feel prompted to inform us about associations their fancy infused in their minds on hearing electronic sounds. This associative force of electronic music seems to stimulate the imagination of the choreographer too.

7. At the risk of seeming to be a partial propagandist, I must point out the practical fact that ballet companies often appear in places where an orchestra cannot be afforded. What happens? The piano accompanist has to play the score, no matter whether it is Tchaikovsky's *Swan Lake* or a complicated modern orchestral score. Such barbarism is impossible with electronic music.

The problem of combining ballets with live orchestral accompaniment and with electronic (loud-speaker) accompaniment in the same programme must be faced. My first experience with such a programme, in the Holland Festival of 1955, was reassuring but at the same time disappointing, as neither the public nor the critics seemed aware of any problem at all. The first experiment of this kind in Germany, at the Hanover Opera, was contemplated with more tension. The choreographer, Yvonne Georgi, offered a programme that started with *Les Sylphides* by Chopin and ended with *Le Loup*, a very colourful ballet, by Henri Dutilleux, both accompanied by symphony orchestra. Between these two, my first electronic ballet was performed, the accompaniment by loudspeakers. All of us who participated in the première, felt it was like a baptism of fire and we came through. None of the critics spoke disdainfully of the loudspeakers; all of them accepted electronic music as equivalent to symphonic music.

Perhaps a severer test was the performance of my second electronic ballet at the Vienna State Opera in 1959. Here the programme included *Les Sylphides*, my ballet *Evolutions*, *Agon* by Stravinsky, and *Ruth*, a ballet première by Heimo Erbse. All of the ballets except mine were accompanied by the famous Vienna Philharmonic Orchestra. The press provided the previews of the programme with nice headlines, such as "Entehrung der heiligen Hallen" (Desecration of the Holy Temple) and "Unmusik in der Staatsoper" (Non-Music at the State Opera). Thus one cannot claim that the test started under favourable conditions for electronic music. The issue was best characterized by the headline over the review in one of the Viennese journals: "Das Tonband siegte" (The Tape Conquered). Without overestimating this, we can state that electronic ballet music is able to stand comparison with symphonic ballet music in the same programme.

SYNTHETIC MEANS

Hugh LeCaine (CANADA)

I would like to make it clear that I am a physicist, not a composer. Perhaps I'm here under false pretences; perhaps you will find it strange to see a physicist on a panel discussing music. However, if this is strange, it's no stranger than the presence of an electronic music studio in a place so august, respectable, I won't say conservative, as the University of Toronto.

If any of you have been to an electronic music studio, I'm sure you will know what I mean. In the first place, if you were to visit the studio during working hours, long before you got there—and, incidentally, working hours are any time during the night or day that the composer happens to feel inspired—long before you got there you would hear the same sound being played over and over again. This is characteristic of an electronic music studio; and it's simply a composer trying to understand the sound, to evaluate it and see what it might be like in connection with other sounds or with transferring replicas of itself. Once inside the door, your first impression would be that the walls were covered with loops of brown ribbon. These are sounds which have been "frozen," just as Rabelais imagined; they can be played back over and over again *ad infinitum*, in fact sometimes *ad nauseam*. On the floor you would see tangled heaps of more or less the same ribbon; these would be sounds transformed by the techniques of electronic music, but sounds which didn't turn out as the composer had intended.

Then, of course, there is the music paper. You'll find the ordinary music paper, with staves printed on the page; but instead of seeing notes on the page, you'll find graphs, little triangles, squares, and all sorts of arcane things, and you will hardly ever find as much as two bars in succession written in the usual way. Besides the music paper, you will find graph paper—which is familiar in an engineering laboratory but not at all familiar in musical surroundings. On the graph paper you will not find graphs, as you would expect. What you will find is that the composer has taken the graph paper, drawn in pencil a musical staff, and proceeded to write down notes in the ordinary musical notation.

It's all very confusing. You might not find a single musical instrument. What you would find would be a great many scientific instruments which look as though they belonged in a nuclear physics lab, or even in the interior of a space-ship as shown on a Grade B motion picture. Very few instruments have been especially developed for the electronic music studio; and this perhaps is why physicists are useful in electronic music.

We are forever being told that this is the age of specialization, but somehow it is a consolation to find that such a close relation exists between science and music. There are definite evidences that music needs science; I almost said that science needs music—it would have sounded very good, but I'm not sure what it would have meant. (However I'm sure that scientists need music, because in some strange way we all have guilty consciences about putting such emphasis on science. There has never been an age when the humanities, and philosophy, and all the studies which have been accepted for years and years, have occupied so little of our attention. Therefore I believe that the average person often feels secretly gratified when he sees some indication that science really fits into aesthetic efforts somewhere.)

As I said, in an electronic music studio the instruments are chiefly those of science, but music's need for science goes a great deal deeper than simply borrowing a few physicists or a few scientific tools. I'm sure you have seen that already in the previous sessions. In respectable periodicals devoted to music, and not necessarily to electronic music exclusively, articles about music appear with titles like these: "Information as a Measure of Structure in Music"; "Twelve-Note Invariants as Compositional Determinants" (two exclusively mathematical terms in the same short title). Then there was "The Elements of Stochastic Music": I'll bet you don't know what "stochastic" is, and I'm not going to tell you. That was in the last *Gravesano Review*. (I don't know what it is either.) We have a new musical vocabulary containing such words as "aleatory." Now "aleatory" I don't mind, because it was such a little-used word that it might as well be taken over by the musicians anyway. But when you come to the anatomical approach which Professor Luening and others have pointed out, and when you find such words as "metabolism" applied to a piece of music, then I really start to wonder. At any rate, these words are an evidence that musicians are forced to—or want to, I don't know which, and that is perhaps an interesting point—anyway, they *do* look at music with a scientific eye. The scientists, of course, look at everything with a scientific eye; it's part of their egocentricity. But musicians are forced, or have wanted, to embrace scientific attitudes and points of view. For instance, a young composer like Karlheinz Stockhausen has taken courses in information theory and communication theory in order to help him understand music better.

This embracing of the scientific point of view may of course be just the age-old desire of artists to use the materials of their time, and this is, well this is not a material, but it's possibly close to it; it leads to the materials. And it may be comparable to sculptors putting down the chisel and taking up the welding torch, or to painters abandoning the brush for the bicycle.

However this may be, it was encouraging in 1954 when the National Research Council, an institution devoted to furthering the annals of science and industry (nothing said about the arts at all), decided to undertake a small programme in the development of electronic instruments for musical use. Now what we have in Ottawa is an electronic music laboratory, and what we hope to do is something similar to what the craftsmen did who developed the violin family. I regret to say that we haven't developed the modern counterpart of the Stradivarius; but we're still trying.

Canada's first electronic music *studio*—that is, the place where musical compositions are actually produced—was opened last year at the University of Toronto. It came into being because of the interest and energy of Dr. Arnold Walter, Director of the Music Faculty of the University of Toronto. In this studio they're working very hard to translate their musical ideas into tape, and to find the direction which seems best suited to this situation. Canadian composers, I believe, as a group, are very much interested in modern music; that is, there are fewer of them than you will find in other countries who want to express themselves in the traditional form. Therefore, it seems reasonable to suppose that they will be eager to experiment with electronic music, and there have been signs of this already.

Now in going over the instruments that we are working on, it is really out of place in this session to refer to anything so old-fashioned as an instrument which is played in time-sequence. However I would like to say that I do have faith that electronic music will solve some of the instrumental problems. If you look at instruments of the orchestra you can see that they are not ideal, and I don't see why the science of electronics, which is an extremely complicated and far-reaching technical body of thought, can't be used to advantage in instruments for the orchestra. An example of a problem which I feel has been solved, which couldn't have been solved apart from electronics, is the touch-sensitive keyboard. The pipe-organ manufacturers have tried many times to put this on a pipe organ but the nature of the sounding bodies in the pipe organ made it impossible to work out a satisfactory control. However, this is a very simple problem in electronics.

There is every advantage apparently in favour of the electronic musical instruments. They can cover a tremendous pitch range; they can cover all the possible timbres in one instrument; they can be played more rapidly than any other instrument, the speed being determined only by the nature of the performer; they have a tremendous amplitude range; and so on. There is only one difficulty: they just don't work. Musically, I mean. And the proof of this is that when you take the best electronic instruments which have ever been developed (and I mean of course the *ondes Martenot*), when you ask one of these instruments to play a simple line, a part or a melody which would have been fascinating and exciting on a simple flute (or, you could go further, on the recorder—even played on a recorder, it would be vital and exciting)—when played on an electronic instrument, it is just deadly dull and flat, insipid. This simply means that musical instruments are very complicated. They take a long time to develop. The fact that we have all these techniques doesn't mean that they will immediately, automatically, produce the useful orchestral instrument. However, I feel that some day there will be an orchestral instrument, using electronics, which will be good enough to be used in both small and large groups.

Electronic music is defined in this fashion. It may use electronic generators of complex wave forms to produce essentially musical sounds, that is, it may use square waves, triangular waves, sawteeth pulses, and so on. It may use such unusual sources as noise generators which, unlike the complex wave forms, don't seem to bear any resemblance to well-known orchestral sounds. It may go further in simplifying sounds: it may use the building-block of complex sounds, which is the sine-wave. These have never before been available in pure form for the composer to experiment with. (For instance, István Anhalt's *Composition no. 3* demonstrates some of the sounds which can be obtained by putting together a large number of sine-waves.) Electronic music may draw its tonal material from the world around us. It may use the sound of a single drop of water, or it may use the sound of the breaking of a pane of glass. These sounds of course have always been with us, but up to date it's never been possible to train them to perform. Now we can do it.

That brings me back to that recorded sound played over and over again, which I said was characteristic of a first impression of an electronic music studio. The very fact that the fleeting and transitory nature of sound has been conquered is extremely important. Now a sound can be criticized, considered, evaluated, can be multiplied and transformed, set at any desired time-relation to itself. The heart of the matter, of course, is the conquest of time. I don't know fully the modern viewpoint on the significance of time. At any rate, electronic composition in this sense is not a strange process—it's exactly what the composer always has been doing when he writes music on music paper. If he writes two sixteenth notes, let's say, they may occur in performance a tenth of a second apart; and yet it may have taken him months after writing the first sixteenth note to think of the second one. Electronic techniques simply make this process, this very same process, practical and possible in terms of the sounds themselves.

The thing that is so interesting is that the composer is brought closer to the sound. This important point of view was the discovery of the *musique concrète* group in France, about 1948. It elevates the recording machine to the status of a musical instrument, and its far-reaching consequences are the last ten years of electronic music. Because of the importance of the tape recorder, I believe it is vital to have a tape recorder designed for music creation alone—not for radio or television, for nuclear physics, or for any other purpose. In a special tape recorder for an electronic music studio, all the musical variables should be in the most convenient form for music. There should be means of handling the short lengths of tape which represent the frozen individual sounds; and this the normal broadcasting-studio recorder is not fit to do, because it's meant for a whole programme, which more or less runs on without the control of the operator. If the tape recorder is controlled by a keyboard, it is important that the keyboard be tunable to any conceivable scale, with as little difficulty as possible. Loudness may be controlled in the individual parts, and they should be capable of being grouped after the model of the orchestra, and slide controls or some of the more conventional controls should be used for slow changes and touch-sensitive keys for rapid ones.

In 1953 Karlheinz Stockhausen surprised the musical world with his *Composition no. 2* in which, for the first time, complete serialization of all the musical parameters was carried out. It's only fair, I suppose, to point out that serialization of all the musical parameters in a piece for orchestra would just be impossible—because they are not under the control of the performer. However, in the case of sine-waves this is possible. Stockhausen realized the far-reaching significance of this, and the interest that there would be in this completely determined music. It certainly is not correct to say that everything has been thought out, because the human mind can't encompass anything completely; but it is possible to say that it was all written down. It all followed from a few simple assumptions, and, as he pointed out in the paper, anybody reading the introduction to the paper could go into the laboratory and produce exactly the same composition. When this composition broke upon the musical world, it had the rather surprising effect of driving people back in the opposite direction to the looser forms of serial writing, where in fact the variables are purposely statistically controlled, instead of events being completely determined. However, the sine-waves were a revelation; and, while I certainly wouldn't use the word "new" sound, I feel that sine-wave composition is the most radical departure from accepted musical practice which has yet been contemplated. Although it is true that in electronic-music compositions the sounds are unfamiliar (at least unfamiliar in a musical context), still they are always reminiscent of, to a greater or lesser extent, well-known sounds. While I certainly don't want to underrate what the tape-recorder method of development can do in changing sounds, it's still not the same thing as taking them completely apart and putting them together again with a synthetic process, that is, the process of going right down to basic materials and assembling them all from there.

Sine-wave composition has established an interesting new direction in electronic music. The people who work with electronic music are extremely industrious. The amount of work required in making electronic music is, to the uninitiated, the person who has never tried it, completely incredible; and this also applies, or perhaps is even more true, in the case of sine-wave compositions, because somewhere, at some point, they have to be handled individually. Because of this, it's interesting to try to consider a more economical means of handling them. Of course, the main thing here is to have an instrument especially designed to do this job, and not, as is being done now, to use instruments designed for something else. Now we are working on a photo-electric control which can call upon any or all of a bank of a hundred sine-wave oscillators which can be tuned anywhere in the audible range. Of course the complete composition is never on one single roll of chart paper, but when you have run the chart through the machine you have the raw material for your composition and it seems to offer unique possibilities, new possibilities, new means of development of musical material.

One problem may seem rather surprising to people who haven't heard a great deal of electronic music. To the uninitiated listener it invariably sounds strange: however, when you listen to it more carefully you find that actually there is less variety than in performances on conventional instruments. This is recognized all over the world, and people are trying various means of elaborating sounds in a way that will be satisfactory, and will make the compositions stand up over a greater number of performances.

For the past two years our electronic music laboratory (not studio) in Ottawa, has had the good fortune of having Professor István Anhalt come to us from the Music Faculty of McGill University for a few months each summer. I am going to play a part of his *Composition no. 3*; what I would like you to listen to is the tonal material. I'm sure even from these short fragments you will be able to hear what he has done in the nature of a plastic control of the tone structure. This plastic control arises from the ability to modify the patterns which are presented to the photo-cell machine, and to produce in an economical way a fine structure. The tones have, as opposed to some electronic compositions, a continuously varying, scintillating quality. I thought when I first heard the composition that these were sounds that I had always wanted to hear. [*Illustration*]

Josef Tal (ISRAEL)

Recently I read a music critic who praised the courage of a young composer who dared to make use of ordinary triads. Are we to infer from this that the application of the serial technique probably means cowardice and electronic music no less than fraud? The informative function of music appears to be in great confusion. The instrument itself is endowed with aesthetic and ethical value; but that which it formulates is neither linguistically conceived, nor as a result of this, linguistically comprehended.

Now I do not believe that we are living in a time of crisis. On the contrary: we are extremely privileged to take part in the productive processes of regeneration of dormant forces, and it is only too understandable that this tremendous task should lead to errors and missteps. None of us is completely sure of the ground—though the philosophy of art may, here and there, shed light on obscurity. All in all the outcome is determined by the unique nature of the organism. This organism develops itself by trial and error. Attentive listening and practical results will bring us further than the careful separation of science and art which is a *contradictio in adjecto*, since there exists no true science without human values and these again are formed by the awareness of underlying facts. Here then is the point of departure for my theme. As for practice, several points may be taken for discussion.

The technical possibilities of the slowly evolving electronic musical instrument lead the imagination of the composer into new ways. These are as different from the traditional paths as perhaps Debussy's musical style is from early polyphonal vocal music. Every composer of electronic music has from his own, as well as from the experience of others, gathered valuable material and this may be the reason for the somewhat over-hasty theorizing and, on the other hand, for the delays in sorting and organizing. I have a strong feeling that now is the time to organize the sequel to Gioseffe Zarlino's *Istitutioni Armoniche*—an *Istitutioni della Musica Electronica*. That is, we must systematically establish combinations of apparent importance, accept, separate, alter, and develop them. Then we shall set up symbols for the chosen formulae and in this way again prepare a sure basis on which future generations may build further without wasting time on polemics. Here follow a few chosen examples for observation as a stimulus for such systematic preparatory work:

In a choreographical composition I had to represent the nervous and hurried flight of a multitude. I renounced every melodic suggestion, and chose in their stead four different timbres (to which I will return again) and, by cutting and repiecing in accordance with more or less well known rules, constructed a fugue, similar to the well-organized representation of disorder on the stage. In this example the effect of the density of time is particularly to be noticed. This is a musical-linguistic phenomenon that comes to its full effect only with the help of tape-cutting. Tone-density is a familiar concept to us, both from the building up of a chord and also from the instrumentation of an orchestral *tutti*. For this latter we have created our traditional symbols after systematic examination. As regards time-density, hitherto only the factors involved in its reproduction have been measured; the phenomenon itself, however, radiates in several directions.

Beethoven has made use to a great extent of active, silent time as opposed to voiced time. We have set up for these mute times the false symbol known as the "pause." The function of these so-called pauses is to linearize time relations. This is based on the recurrence of pauses during linear time. In addition, we are now able to produce electronically the most rapid variations in time with a precision which has hitherto been unobtainable. These are added to the timbre characteristic of the basic tone and produce finally, by a combination of vertical and horizontal relationships, a frequency structure where individual organisms are absorbed into serving the whole.

It follows from this suggestion that a systematic number of experiments may lead to a formulation of ideas from which the composer may choose and elaborate suitable tone material. Such a sound, coming in this way from a number of sources, is indeed to be found in every score of a Ravel and indeed, based on this tradition, we should gain sufficient knowledge and confidence to be able to find our way in a more or less intelligent manner in the new area of electronic music.

In one of my works I bring the human voice into contact with the electronic apparatus. It is known that we are able to change the voice until it is unrecognizable, in the hope that we may derive new qualities from it. The words of biblical text, recited in litany, are as follows:

> *And the Lord went before them by day in a pillar of a cloud,*
> *to lead them the way; and by night in a pillar of fire,*
> *to give them light; to go by day and night:*
> *He took not away the pillar of the cloud by day, nor the*
> *pillar of fire by night, from before the people.*

To the words "cloud" and "fire" I have given a musical interpretation which, for the word "cloud," adds to the reciting voice an oriental micro-tone-structure with the help of mechanical time-extension; and for the word "fire," transposed and cut curves of the singing voice. I am quite aware of the fact that I have discovered nothing new in this. But on the other hand exercises in composition in this direction may develop an electronic choir passage which may introduce organic and electronic possibilities to counterpoint.

We may consider the extremely important question of electronic tone-production. Since tones are produced with oscillators in a simple manner and are easily controllable by metering, it is also easy to modify electronically recorded tones of mechanical instruments. With these, the composer may come upon some very interesting surprises, often to be proved only afterward upon analysis. I have, by placing a pick-up upon the sound boxes of various musical instruments and recording the resultant tone with a microphone, achieved certain sounds, the synchronous recording of which produces a minor triad as a result of the specific overtone dynamics. But the resultant tone is dependent on so many coincidences that I could not perform the experiment a second time without achieving totally different results. With sine-tones and combinations thereof one is on safe ground. This convenience, however, means a total rejection of undetermined elements. Schopenhauer said that justice is like that chemical substance which can never be made in the completely pure state, but only alloyed with some impurity. I believe that this is also valid here.

We must ask ourselves what we chiefly demand from an electronic tone. We can make a religion of the purity of the sine-tone, we can use "white noise" as a counterpart, but we cannot shut our ears to the fact that, compared with conventional tone material, as the bearer of sound content, electronic tone material is inherently narrower and more rigid; indeed it has the characteristics of synthetic material. This acknowledgement brings us to a delicate situation. For naturally the sound of conventional instruments may be synthesized electronically with tremendously complex machinery. But is has been justly stated that this is not the function of electronic music. However, there is not nearly enough tone material at our disposal for electronic music for us to dispose of the conventional. Therefore there came quite early the ideologically distorted necessity of searching for the new, the never-heard, the originality *à tout prix* that always leads rapidly to complete sterility.

Not so very long ago this voracity for the new in the modern orchestral palette so misled the composer as to preclude him from devising an instrumental theme which could also be played on other instruments. Then again the instrument was considered an end in itself. I find in an essay by Donald Francis Tovey an extremely applicable statement: "This is as much as to argue that no gentleman should say anything that could possibly be said by a lady and no lady should say anything that could possibly be said by a gentleman."

We know very well that this thirst after originality includes all parameters. If we are to pursue our course in peace, our elementary concern in the production of electronic tones must be in the realm of the possibility of controlling the individual components with financially feasible and aesthetically satisfying projects. Should, in addition, similarities with the known tones of other intruments appear, I for one will not be distressed, so long as these tones are necessary for the creation of the composition and represent points of departure for further electronic development. Such imitation of sound appears in altogether new relationships in specific recording techniques which cannot be accomplished with conventional playing (here I refer particularly to Dr. Hugh LeCaine's "Creative Tape Recorder"). On the basis of such considerations, our engineer, Mr. Fred Goldwater, was commissioned to build a tone generator, working on the well-known principle of the optical siren, but providing, in its details, specific possibilities for electronic composition. Here is Mr. Goldwater's description of the instrument:

"Some of the requirements for the ideal artificial (electronic) musical tone generator may be easily summarized. The instrument should be capable of generating musical tones of continuously varying pitch, easily adjustable: the number and harmonic relationship of the overtones should be as flexible as possible and the level of each overtone variable; the output level of the complete tone should be subject to direct control; and the entire instrument should be suitable for the production of various tones with a minimum of simple, straightforward and repeatable readjustments.

"Before the construction of the instrument, some of the many possible methods of generating tones were considered with reference to the foregoing requirements. These included: the phonic wheel, the use of oscillators tuned individually to the required harmonic frequencies, a "saw-tooth" or other oscillator rich in harmonic content from which the individual harmonics could be abstracted by filters, and simultaneous generation of all desired overtones by some electro-mechanical method. The phonic wheel, involving the design of a 'wave-form pattern' for each tone, was rejected as lacking flexibility. Oscillators to be tuned individually to harmonic frequencies would require the utmost refinement in design and the use of stable precision components. The difficulty of tuning such oscillators would preclude simple, rapid changes both in frequency and in tone structure. The saw-tooth oscillator, to be used with filters, would require a complex of expensive electronic components and would also require considerable manipulation when changing either the frequency or structure of the tone.

"The simplest form of an electro-mechanical method for the simultaneous generation of all overtones—based on the interruption of the light falling upon phototubes—was therefore selected.

"Let me describe the operation of the instrument. Several rows of different numbers of holes are provided in a disc rotated by a variable speed meter. For each row of holes there is a lamp and phototube combination. The electrical impulse generated by interruption of the light falling on the phototube is amplified—a separate amplifier with individual gain control and an electronic phase shifter allowing nearly 360° of phase angle adjustment being provided for each phototube. These features allow adjustment of the magnitude and the phase angle for each component of the complete tone, independently and simply. Ordinary pointer knobs and dials indicate the settings so that any previously developed tone may be reproduced at will.

"The electrical signals from each channel are mixed together electronically and, in addition to a master gain control, several additional features are provided to allow the generation of tones whose output level varies in accordance with a preset pattern. This is accomplished by means of a keyed amplifier, the gain of which is controlled by two one-shot multivibrators in association with various resistance-capacitance networks. These elements make possible a tone which builds up from silence to a predetermined initial 'attack' level at a controllable rate; continues at this level a definite length of time; decays to a lower, continuous "tone" level at a present rate; continues at this level a further interval of time; and then decays in silence. Each of the characteristics of this tone-build-up time, 'attack' level, 'attack' time, decay time to 'tone' level, 'tone' duration, and final decay to silence is individually controllable, allowing complete manipulation of the various aspects of the tone and repetition whenever desired."

There is no doubt these are but the raw beginnings, comparable to the "zinks" of the sixteenth century. We must nevertheless keep our vision unclouded so as not to fall into the net of pseudo-science, where all the aliveness of indeterminacy will be lost. It must be the musician who demands from the designer the instrument he requires. And when these instruments are built, the Gordian knots of all art philosophies of electronic music will naturally come untied.

Vladimir Ussachevsky (USA)

It appears that while the medium of electronic music, in common with many musical advances of the past, has reached the point where its potential for survival seems well assured, the danger of the subject being talked to death is clearly with us. In my own case I became aware of this danger in the summer of 1960 when, following my talk on electronic music before the Convention of the American Symphony League, I next delivered twelve hours of lectures concerning music in tape medium to a class at the University of Colorado, and then proceeded to the Composers' Conference at Stratford with a similar purpose. Economic and publicity purposes aside, a composer who forsakes his tape recorder for a typewriter or a lectern is in one way succumbing to the inevitable necessity of propagandizing or defending his efforts. In doing so he is following in the historical footsteps of many composers, and, in common with them, he frequently shares the traditional uneasiness that to entrust an evaluation of his work solely to critical opinion may be precarious. Nevertheless, if he is free of a Messianic complex, a composer knows that in some respects it is premature to think that he has formulated judgments of lasting significance. The potential of the electronic medium is so vast that it is more important right now to parallel the rise of public interest with a proportionate growth of new compositions sufficiently varied in styles and materials to demonstrate the enormous richness of sounds and the opportunities for structural ingenuity with new materials. Even then, there certainly is already more than ample evidence that the existing interest in electronic music transcends mere curiosity. The emotional and the intellectual involvement demonstrated by all types of audiences indicates that enduring values are present in the many compositions from the growing repertoire of the various schools.

From the foregoing it must be clear that I do not propose to engage in polemics—especially on the subject of whether electronic music is a branch of serious musical art or, as some would like to question, whether it has anything to do with music at all. Similarly I shall avoid technical explanations of processes employed in the tape medium; though I shall briefly speak of the ways in which material played on the tape recorder is synchronized with the orchestra. The following remarks, rather, attempt to answer some of the questions frequently raised, and so may help to clarify the *raison d'être* of electronic music.

Does electronic music represent "mechanization of an art"? Nonsense! The combination of machines which are used to produce electronic music simply constitutes a new instrument. The technique acquired to manipulate various parts of this instrument is bent towards making the precise machines serve the imagination in the most exacting way possible. The reward is a chance to exercise, with greatly increased sensitivity, direct control over the sound material from its raw stage to finished form. Yet, let no one think that machines make the task of producing a composition simpler. They do not unless one is willing to settle for clichés and entrust the selection of sound material and all structural organization almost completely to the particular properties of the machine itself.

The task cannot be anything but more complex since, I repeat, electronic music represents further development into sensitivity, and a lesser rather than a greater tendency toward creative mechanization.

What is the optimum way in which electronic music can be developed? Of course, it must derive from a background of musical ideas. Subtleties of rhythm and timbre can be handled with the utmost sophistication. Compositions so carefully nurtured will certainly require a high degree of sophistication from listeners.

Undeniably a strong temptation, and by no means sinful, is to make use of bizarre juxtapositions, dramatic outbursts, and out-of-this-world sounds which can be created with comparative ease. The purists raise the cry that such doings remove electronic music from the realm of pure music. My answer to this is: Let any ten persons agree on what constitutes "pure music" or even just "music." If we are so anxious to preserve the purity of the art—an art which has survived every instrumental innovation and bizarre use thereof by composers—let us then hope that it may not lose its vitality through loss of opportunity for metamorphosis and expansion.

I emphatically believe that one of the important tasks facing electronic music is to extract the musical potential from the wide variety of sound materials which are mostly non-instrumental and non-musical in origin. The range and vastness of these resources increase the composer's responsibility to organize his composition especially along abstract lines. Novelty of sound is transitory. To create electronic music requires not less but rather more musical training, plus some extra-musical knowledge as well. Thus the optimum way of developing electronic music depends upon familiar prerequisites: the imagination and skill of the composer, availability of proper tools (in this case, electronic tools) and of proper performing conditions.

What are these proper performing conditions? One is inclined to doubt that a conventional concert hall is the ideal place. A few special halls with multiple loudspeaker systems should be available adjacent to the centres of electronic music. Advantage of such existing proximity is now being taken in the McMillin Theater of Columbia University where one of the studios of the Columbia-Princeton Electronic Music Center is located a short distance from the stage and the auditorium. An installation of nineteen loudspeakers distributed in 360° around the auditorium is now being completed. Eventually a maximum of twelve separate sound sources can be fed to these loudspeakers. Through experiments and actual performances we hope to obtain exhaustive verification of a premise that controlled movement of one or several sound patterns significantly enhances the effect of a composition in the electronic medium. In addition we shall attempt to determine the pertinent information about particular acoustical conditions in order that the composer may use this opportunity to incorporate movement of sound intelligently as a part of a structural design in his composition. It is hoped that, in this type of performance, carefully planned distribution of tensions, combined with the opportunities for complete dynamic control, and the possibilities for precise juxtaposition of harmonic masses and polyphonic lines, may make up for that loss of aural and visual excitement which enhances the pleasure of listening to an orchestral performance.

Incidentally, a somewhat misunderstood but, in my opinion, a perfectly legitimate area of expanding the advantages of electronic media is in conjunction with an orchestra. The employment of a tape recorder as a solo instrument gives rise to the obvious problem of how it is to be synchronized with the orchestra. The principal limitation to be overcome is obviously that of the present inability of any tape recorder to modify, at a conductor's command, the tempo of the solo part on tape without raising or lowering the pitch. (Surprisingly, a device to accomplish this exists, but it is far from perfect.) This limitation can be overcome if a composer gives it due consideration in the conceptual stages of his work. In a way it is not any more difficult to plan around this limitation than to consider the necessity of giving players of wind instruments opportunities to take a breath, or refraining from impossible ranges or speeds of execution from performers. My colleague, Otto Luening, and I have been fortunate to have been able to prove this point by incorporating a tape recorder as a solo instrument in three symphonic works commissioned by three different symphony orchestras. Professor Luening has also fulfilled a commission for a ballet using orchestra and a tape recorder. All told, over twenty performances of these works have been given by major symphony orchestras in the United States, Belgium, and South America. This seems to indicate that the combination of a tape recorder and a symphony orchestra can be a fruitful one, and interest in audiences and among musicians is excited not so much by the novelty of this combination as by the discovery that this union of an electronic instrument and the orchestra serves not to *diminish* but to *enrich* the palette of orchestral sounds. In its long and glorious history, the orchestra has either absorbed or rejected countless instruments, but never before has it been possible to employ an instrument which is capable of reproducing sounds taken from the total world of natural or synthesized sounds.

In composing a work for tape recorder and orchestra, one has to decide which portion of the sound material must synchronize precisely with the orchestra and then compose that portion of the work in such a manner as to provide the conductor with the cues. Several methods may be employed. A musical passage played on tape is composed to appear in advance of an orchestral entrance, but in a tempo which is to be followed without modification when the orchestra comes in. This method can be successfully relied upon during the close antiphonal exchanges between the tape and the orchestra, as well as at the end or in the middle of an extended tape solo when the orchestra is brought in after so many measures of rest. Somewhat less flexible, but also practical, is to have the orchestra follow the tempo of the tape for one to three minutes in a type of music which inherently requires rhythmic rigidity.

Normally, a tape recorder is stopped several times during the course of one composition while the orchestra plays alone. Bringing in a tape recorder on cue is no particular problem. The silent portion of the tape is carefully marked with a line and an arrow, and this line is placed exactly in the middle of the playback head of the tape recorder. The tape is usually started from three to six seconds in advance of the actual entrance in the score.

It is very useful to compose a certain portion of a work for tape recorder and orchestra so as to allow either the tape part or the orchestra to enter with a leeway of a second or two. This lack of precise synchronization may be carried further through any number of measures in those cases when the timbre and rhythmic nature of sound material is so complex as to be not readily comprehensible. This planned random juxtaposition gives the conductor the opportunity to maintain a flexibility of tempo without being concerned about the tape part.

Choosing wisely between the precise and the random a composer can avoid the necessity of compromising his musical ideas. On the contrary, several unprecedented opportunities are at his disposal. Almost unlimited rhythmic complexity can be obtained in combining the material on tape with the orchestra, especially since the main burden of complexity can be imposed on the prepared tape part. Rich new timbres as well as pure noise spectrum blend surprisingly well with the conventional instrumental sounds. It is my opinion that imaginatively conceived and properly used sound material on tape will not only enrich the total sound picture obtained from the orchestra-and-tape combination, but will allow for the liberation of some orchestral instruments from routine tasks which they are frequently obliged to perform in the ordinary orchestral score. So liberated, they can be used for some unusual combinations among themselves. I advocate this as a largely untried field of exploration, and at the same time wish to emphasize that it is quite wasteful in time and futile in many other ways to try to duplicate the orchestral instruments on tape.

A good deal of what I have just described has been employed in the two commercially recorded compositions done jointly by Otto Luening and myself, *Rhapsodic Variations for Tape Recorder and Orchestra* and *Poem in Cycles and Bells*.

I should like to stress that there are no mysteries in this medium that will not succumb to the good musical sense which is the common property of all thoughtful and open-minded composers. In all fairness one must mention that there are obstacles yet to be overcome. The principal difficulties are with the availability of the technical facilities—a problem which can be solved only gradually. Commercially the new medium is handicapped by the traditional inflexibility of media which potentially could use what electronic music has to offer to a considerable advantage. On the other hand, there has been a gratifying response from audiences; one is also inclined to believe that, in common with a good deal of contemporary music, electronic music already appears to have been immunized by repeated injections of criticism. This alone assures it a place in the next edition of Mr Nicolas Slonimsky's *Lexicon of Musical Invective*. The important fact is that electronic music is attracting increasing attention from young composers everywhere in the world; that its appearance on the musical scene is timely; and that, stripped of the strait jacket of premature dogma, it can offer a new stimulus to the imagination and provide a thread that can lead out of the labyrinth of the usual choices which more often than not terminate in the graveyard of the neo-past.

Discussion

Edgard Varèse (USA): Just one thing I would like to say, speaking of the relation of art and science: it's not something very new, because in the Middle Ages we had the two branches of knowledge, the *trivium* and the *quadrivium*, the one being the art of language and the other one being the art of science; and in the second one, the *quadrivium*, we had arithmetic, geometry, astronomy, and music. So consequently from the beginning of the Middle Ages the scientific aspect of music was always considered.

Luciano Berio (ITALY): Mr LeCaine was talking about problems of instrumental music, instruments, and so on. I strongly believe that instruments do not make any problem by themselves: the problem is with the musicians. Instruments are invented and evolve because of the musical thought, and not by themselves.

An observer (USA): Is it necessary, in the combination of electronic music and conventional instruments, to be so obvious rhythmically in order to keep the conductor informed of where the tape is? Is it not possible for humans to hear more involved sounds on tape? I've heard a work by Henri Pousseur which combines these two mediums and seems to do so with very sophisticated musical matter in both electronic and conventional instruments. Does the conductor and do the musicians have great problems in the performance of such a work?

Otto Luening (USA, *chairman*): I think the degree of difficulty in which you want to engage is mostly a matter of what you are doing it for. You can, of course, write a kind of co-ordination that would be extremely complex; maybe given enough rehearsal time you could do that. It *is* a matter of rehearsal time—and also how good your conductor is.

Berio: I think it's very much a problem of the *type* of co-ordination. If we require a rhythmical co-ordination or metrical co-ordination, typical of tonal music for instance, we are obliged to give very simple, very clear cues. But the piece by Pousseur is much different. Usually we tend to give a geometrical design to our musical experience. In electronic music, for good and systematic reasons, we usually say the simplest indivisible element is the sinus wave, and the most complex is "white noise." That means you have less information with the sinus wave, and more information with white noise; you have less meaning with the sinus wave and more meaning with white noise. But the two geometrical limits are not important; it's what's between—and what's between can be discovered in a very free way each time. The piece by Pousseur is not a case of a very rhythmical co-ordination by the two sources, the recorded source and the live source. But at the beginning of the composition there is a possibility of co-ordinating in groups of sounds all the musical events, and the continuity between the two sound-productions, the live one and the recorded one, is so carefully worked out that it can very well support even more than two or three seconds of shifting.

A questioner asked for a definition of the term "white noise."

LeCaine: This is generated by electronic processes involving a large number of individual units, not actually electrons but something getting down to that size. Usually it's avoided like the plague. It's a record scratch, background noise in radio, and so on. The interesting thing about it musically is its relation to the chance event and randomness; and possibly the most surprising thing, as you just heard, is that it contains the maximum possible amount of information. The musical associations? I don't know; I think I'll just not say anything about that; let somebody else comment on that.

Ussachevsky: When you speak of white noise you speak of the total spectrum. On very few occasions would you use that in its pure form. You usually take bands of this noise, which means that you simply select certain areas of this spectrum. The closest comparable effect you could obtain, in connection with a musical instrument, would be putting your fist, say, between middle C on the piano and the G above it, plus all the black and white notes and even that kind of a cluster would still be entirely too definite as compared to white noise. But you can, if you want to, by a filtering of white noise, obtain very definite pitch areas. In fact, you can obtain something that is only two or three frequencies; and in this respect you get a new colour, very useful for some of the percussive effects, very useful if you reverberate it; and in this manner, depending upon whether you want to have definite pitches or just definite wide pitch areas, you can use white noise in any way which suits your fancy.

Louis Applebaum (CANADA): We know that various countries of the world are setting up laboratories for the investigation of electronic music. To what degree are these studios open to composers who wish to involve themselves in this process of investigation?

Berio: An electronic studio is very expensive; you must pay technicians, engineers, musicians; and in fact these studios are always attached to radio stations, universities or big industries. So this prevents, in a way, a young musician from using the studio as a musician uses an orchestra (which is now much more available than a studio). Then besides this fact, there is a bureaucratic aspect, which in our society is usually attached to anything higher than a certain financial level. That means for a musician to come to a studio, say, in Milan, to work, he must write to the Italian radio. If this musician makes his demand officially, being backed by influential people, he can have a very good hope of coming to this studio. But if he makes the demand as a private individual, he can be sure he will be refused; and I think this can be applied to other studios, generally speaking.

Luening: I would like to say something about the Columbia-Princeton studio, which is a little bit different. We are under the auspices of two universities, and we do have our academic bureaucracy which we have to circumvent in order to get things going sometimes. But we have succeeded so far, in the studio, in opening it up to a number of people. For instance, Varèse works there; he is one of the partners in the enterprise. We have Milton Babbitt; and Ussachevsky and myself. We have had composers from Italy, from Turkey, from Egypt, from Japan, from the University of California, the University of Illinois—considering the fact that we are pretty crowded, we try to be as hospitable as the traffic will bear. Like rehearsal time, you have also to consider studio time.

Berio: We should add that in the case of a studio belonging to a radio station the station wants, and also has the right, to use the studio as a mass-production means, to produce background music and many such things which are very useful for radio. So only one or two musicians at a time, each month, can work in a radio studio.

Ussachevsky: There are certain problems which are peculiar to any studio. Problem number one: Is the composer, who is going to come, already acquainted with some of the techniques, or does he have to start from scratch? If he has to start from scratch, then you have to give him full technician's time. You have to indoctrinate him beforehand, and so forth. Secondly, of course, a composer who is using a studio, whether it is a studio that contains $5,000 worth of equipment or $150,000 worth, is occupying that studio for that time—and it's not available to anyone else. So the number of composers that you can accommodate will always depend on these possibilities of a technician's help and the availability of studio space. I think that in connection with educational institutions there are programmes already being initiated. Mr Badings told me about Utrecht; and Columbia has already started giving some training to people who are interested in general in musical-acoustical problems, some of whom may want to have a crack at working in the studio. In other words, we are also in the process, but we are not ready yet to prepare the so-called indoctrination materials, because it is one thing to let a person sit down and listen to the repertoire of every studio—Milan studio, Cologne, *musique concrète*, Columbia-Princeton, and so forth—but it's quite another to *teach* him how to do it. It is in that area that a certain slowness comes in.

Jean Papineau-Couture (Canada) raised a new point. In his view, there was in electronic music a constant over-charging of the loudspeakers with sound. He compared the experience to a meal where all courses would be served simultaneously.

Varèse: Well, you could say the same thing of certain singers, who think they are very good if they yell.

Berio: Here's an important thing: in electronic music the sound is very far from being so rich, so interesting, as instrumental sound. In our compositions we try instinctively to overcome this by giving much more richness to *all* the parameters of sound. In a way, also, the loudness at which instinctively we play electronic music could be regarded as a compensation for the less rich quality of the sound—besides the fact that the sinus wave is very tiring to hear, extremely tiring, much more tiring to hear than a fortissimo of full orchestra, which is so very rich. A fortissimo of electronic music, which would by actual measuring be no more loud than a fortissimo of orchestra, gives you the impression of fatiguing you much more. For this reason, it is absolutely necessary every time we listen publicly to electronic music to have a proper stereophonic apparatus—not to have a unidirectional source of sound, but at least four or five loudspeakers well distributed in the hall: because the structure of the music involves also its space-distribution. When you have a cheap or medium-quality reproduction system, you are very easily disturbed.

Tal: I know from my own experience that one educates oneself in time to listen to the sounds and to detect a lot of details. Theoretically, if you had played to people of the third century the Ninth Symphony of Beethoven, possibly they would have listened only to some white noise—because they were not educated to understand or analyse such a lot of different acoustical appearances; and here it is very similar. I wouldn't agree that loudness can substitute for some real content in music. If it is only loudness, it wouldn't say very much. But loudness is here connected with a very complex sound, and the moment you are able to analyse the complexity of the sound and to detect all the different colours in it, and they may have a really co-ordinated meaning, then the sound says the same thing as a *tutti* in an orchestra.

Karl-Birger Blomdahl (SWEDEN): Now you have begun to talk about the things I think are very crucial and very important in this whole discussion. Let's be a little more precise. For instance, I question the basic possibility of the electronic means, as we use them now, as bearers of really rich musical ideas, because of their basic poorness of expression—as Mr Berio has just said.

Berio: I didn't say that!

Blomdahl: No, no! I know. But I'm drawing some consequences of this. For, to me, let's say, a French horn or an English horn, has a sound—a basic, elementary sound—and the sound is that much richer than practically all the so-called complex sounds that we can make now with our electronic machinery, that for me, for instance, when I am choosing the means I want to work with, for artistic purposes, I find still the conventional apparatus offers much more. I believe in the future of the electronic means, but I still think they are so primitive. For instance, when listening to the mixture of electronic music and the conventional orchestra, as soon as the electronic music comes in the level of expression (I'm speaking of expression, not of loudness, because loudness is one factor that, in a way, is very superficial), the level of expressiveness goes down, for me, very much.

Berio: I was talking simply of physical richness, which has nothing to do with the musical richness. Vocal music is much richer in this sense than instrumental music, because what happens in the human voice is unbelievable, fascinating; sometimes it can only be seen in a statistical way. That doesn't mean that vocal music is richer in expression than instrumental music. From the moment I make a choice—as a musician I must make a choice—I must justify my choice in a musical work. So if I use electronic sounds I must justify them, their characteristics, with my musical work. The concept doesn't exist any more, of a "rich" or a "poor" sound; it's just the idea of composing that gives sounds their quality.

Blomdahl: You don't have to explain this to me. I would never write a symphony for an accordion.

Luening: It seems to me we have hit the area of psycho-acoustics, of the ear itself. Here we've had a little duet by these two distinguished gentlemen that shows that opinions differ on this subject. A great deal of exploration probably has to be made. It *is* being made, by some of us who sit for hours trying to figure out the next balance which would be good for a certain piece, and on this basis choose it—perhaps rightly, perhaps wrongly—and not to everybody's taste immediately. I think this matter of what goes on in the balance—whether the quality is poorer or richer, and so on—I certainly think that it enters into our minds as we work on this material. I know I modify my own taste by *practising*, by going through ear-training in the electronic sounds, in my particular electronic sounds. It's on the basis of *that* that I come to some sort of selection, which someone maybe doesn't like, but possibly can identify. Perhaps that's already somewhat of a contribution: if you can spot what you don't like.

LeCaine: Could I ask what is the meaning of musical material? How can musical material have meaning before it has been composed? Surely the meaning is in the composition. How could a French horn sound be meaningful?

Blomdahl: I didn't say that. I only said it's so much richer.

LeCaine: What do you mean by "richer"? Richer in what?

Blomdahl: It seems to me so much more complex.

LeCaine: Why should it be helpful in expressing a musical meaning simply because it is more complex? This is an extremely important point!

Blomdahl: Well, after all—well, it appeals to my imagination. . . .

LeCaine: Ah, that's the key!

Blomdahl: . . . through the ear to my imagination. I think that is the starting-point for every composer. He has to hear some sound that goes through the ear to his brain, starts his imagination. The sounds must be—they must simply start me off; they must be rich enough to set my imagination to work.

Luening: It's really time to go to lunch.

FORM

Vagn Holmboe (DENMARK). *On Form and Metamorphosis*

Curiously enough, the dualism of the last century is still generally considered the natural basis for our ideas about form, in that one principally distinguishes between ideas like *substance* and *form*. In order to undertake an analysis, such distinguishing is naturally practical, even necessary, but one must not forget that this analysis is not an examination of musical reality (the reality which only exists in the dimension of time) and that the analysis has to express itself in a symbolic way on the basis of a number of written notes. Naturally, the background for analysis is the knowledge about musical experiences one has had in former days, and experiences of musical reality one expects to meet with in the future—which, however, does not make the analysis itself more real.

At this point, I want to say at once that by form I naturally do not mean the well-known formal frame, which we know from the baroque fugue or the classical sonata and rondo. Just such a scheme has in later times been considered a duality in regard to musical substance, nearly as if the form was identical with the famous bottle, the content of which can be changed according to the taste, demand, and ideals of different periods.

When, in our time, one feels forced to leave this dualism, there are several reasons, reasons which again must be sought outside the musical world, for instance in natural science, psychology, and sociology. To a musician, however, the purely musical tendencies must be decisive. Because one abandons the thought about duality between the musical substance and the musical form, the two things will not automatically become identical. Substance is not form, and form is not substance. On the other hand, one can say that form principally *is* substance, but realized in time—or, in other words, that substance looked upon in the dimension of time necessarily becomes form. Whether it is good or bad form, whether it is what we call perfect form or formless, amorphous or organic, are aesthetic considerations of no importance to the question. If one wants in a simple way to characterize the term substance, it must be something like this: tones or sounds in different pitch (precisely or imprecisely), based on tonality, modality, the twelve-tone system or any other system, realized in any sound-factor (vocal, instrumental, electronic, or concrete), and worked out functionally, by thematic, unthematic, motivic, serial, or any other means imaginable. But already such working-out of motives or series crosses the border-line between pure substance and substance in the dimension of time—in other words, form.

The length and quality of the different tones and sounds, the distance of time between them and between important points in the musical work—in other words, rhythm, metre, agogic elements, and dynamics—belong to those components which directly constitute form. Those components we are naturally able to analyse from a given picture of notes. It can be useful in the notes to examine the place and the mutual relations of the different components, to measure distances and count notes, bars, or series; but that will never be analysis of the music itself, only of its symbols; such analysis does not tell you how the music is perceived, when it exists in the dimension of time.

On the other hand, one can say that when a musical work is heard, when it is experienced in time, analytical considerations about the substance will invariably influence the experience of time itself—which means the experience of musical form. Therefore, the relation between the static substance and the moved substance—in other words between material and form—becomes complementary in the sense that substance and form at the same time complete and exclude each other.

There seems here to be a similarity with the situation in atomic science, when an examination of the electrons of the atoms is the question. The electrons are, from one point of view, particles, but from another point of view they appear like waves, a fact which Niels Bohr calls complementary in the sense in which I have employed the word. It is, by the way, hardly in natural science alone that one finds this harmony, but also in other branches of science, for instance in biology and psychology. And behind this harmony lies an ardent desire in the human being to find unity in things, to find entirety, and, further, a comprehension of time as dimension. We must go as far back as the Renaissance to find a similar situation. At that time, space was acknowledged as a dimension, and at the same time one found one's way forward to perspective in the art of painting, and functional harmony in music.

If music is to have any meaning at all to the human being, to the listener, there must be a certain balance between the essential points in a work, and between the different elements of the work. This balance is found standardized in the historical formal patterns (a balance which has most often been reached through the intensive work of generations). But just this balance, given in advance, will influence the living relation between substance and form. It will force the substance to standardization, which will make it stiff, and create a dualism between substance and form. Such dualism will almost invariably result in a conflict between substance and form, or in a pastiche-like adjustment to a given formal scheme.

Therefore any development or change of the musical substance sooner or later must be followed by a change or development of the musical form, which then, in the course of time, stiffens in concrete patterns and schemes. For, I repeat, musical form is in principle nothing but the latent possibilities of substance realized in the dimension of time.

At the present time many different composers are working with the problems of substance, and simultaneously with the problems of form. I need only draw your attention to the many efforts in contemporary music, trying to find new means of expression, covering points from extreme spontaneity to extreme determinism. Still, a generally acknowledged principle of form does not seem to have been created, as for example the fugue at the time of Bach or the sonata at the time of Haydn and Mozart. But there are indications that a process of crystallizing already is at work, and that composers from several sides, at different places, and within many musical attitudes, more or less consciously are heading for the same goal. This goal seems at the present moment to be the realization of one or several *forms of unity*—or, more correctly, there are so many tendencies to monistic formal feeling that one imagines a future common goal.

The principle of variation is old, but it holds a very important place in twelve-tone music as in modal and tonal music—so important that we probably have to go back to the varied unity-forms of the baroque era to find something similar. Twelve-tone music and serialism are likewise in principle monistic, and already in the first works of Schoenberg within the twelve-tone system one feels that form is a serious problem. The conventional twelve-tone music can, so to speak, be adapted to any kind of formal scheme; but, in spite of this fact, twelve-tone music has a tendency, according to its own nature (that is, the twelve tones and the four aspects of the series: basic series, inversion, retrograde series, and retrograde-inversion), a tendency towards variable courses. Quite a number of ideas—mutation, permutation, aspects, prisms, facets, perspective, metamorphosis—are characteristic expressions for different efforts within contemporary music, and at the same time they are names for some of the formal possibilities latent either in one substance-complex, in one series, or in one musical centre of form.

I want to concentrate on one of these ideas, namely metamorphosis, which partly is already of a certain importance, and partly is a principle of form with quite special possibilities for contemporary music. And this not least for serial music, whether the series is orthodox twelve-tone or based more on modal factors.

Speaking about metamorphosis as a principle of form, I do not in any way mean a formal scheme. In reality, I doubt whether a special metamorphic form has yet been created, such as we know from the sonata or rondo of former days. And as it mainly will be a question of quantity whether or not such a form has already been established, it is of no great interest to these principal considerations.

What the word metamorphosis means is well known, and I need only here refer to biology, where the word covers, to take one example, the development from egg, caterpillar, and pupa to the fully grown insect. The word is also used in a psychologic-symbolic way, in the well-known myth about the phoenix, the bird which feels its strength failing and therefore flies straight into the fire, where it burns and rises again out of the ashes.

From a musical point of view there seem to be relations between metamorphosis and variation or a certain part of the classical sonata. I do not here want to look into possible historical lines of development—that would, without doubt, be both premature and too uncertain—but I shall, on the contrary, say a few words about the conditions which make it clear that the metamorphic principle is not bound up with other principles of form.

Metamorphosis is, for natural reasons, based on a principle of unity. With a starting-point less in a theme than in a complex of motives, rhythms, and sounds, or in a series, be it twelve-tone or modal, or in recognizable electronic or concrete elements—with such a starting-point, the transforming of elements which takes place will be understood and experienced as a metamorphosis. Further, it is not sufficient to have merely a side-by-side placing of basic idea and transformation. A development must take place and this development must be characterized by a strong logic; whether one or several transformations take place, and whether the changes take place by stages or in one single continuous whole are factors of no concern here. Every part of the process must appear as an absolute necessity, and possibly by increasing degrees point towards the final transformation.

To illustrate this, I shall quote the composer Karl-Birger Blomdahl, who, in some comments about his Third Symphony (*Facets*) of 1950, says: "Theme with variations! The classical form? No!—that is too schematic and static. It has to be an organic form of variations, which grows from inside. Out of itself. Always changing—always new—always the same—always new—always the same—always new—."

The development mentioned can of course be formed in different ways according to the latent demands in the chosen substance. To go into details in this question is difficult, as one is apt very easily to cross the borderline between the principle of form and concrete form. However, I have to add a more subjective consideration, based on experiences from my work with metamorphosis on modal and modal-serial bases. It seems to me that the process can take place in two ways: either through a continuous development by which one aspect gradually joins the other, or through a complete working-up of the basic substance, a spending of all its possibilities, an atomizing of its forces in such a way that a metamorphosis according to circumstances becomes a logical solution both in regard to substance and psychologically.

Now I hope that this short and incomplete survey makes it fairly clear that metamorphosis is a principle just as different from variations, sonata and fugue, as these principles are mutually different.

Employing schemes—in substance as well as formally—is

naturally in many ways a facility to the composer. In any case, the formal schemes are normally so well worn that the composer's greatest problem will be how to cut his stuff to suit his scheme, or, as it is written in the fairy tale about Cinderella: "Cut a heel and clip a toe, and the shoe fits."

Metamorphosis is still not a fixed form (and I do not hope that it will become so in my time). It has no absolute scheme; it is only a principle, but possesses a variability and plasticity which make it quite specially useful, as well for serial as for non-serial music. And just because it has no pre-determined proportions, the problem of time must invariably play a big role, just as would be the case with all other kinds of music which do not depend on formal schemes.

We all know that what we could call musical time is not the same as astronomical time. Music creates in different ways its own time, which cannot, as a matter of course, be measured by means of a clock. We also know that musical time is not a fixed unity, but that it is decided by the idea of psychological time, which again decides the form-experience of the listener (and I take it for granted that music must be heard). Thus a listener will normally feel that very intensive or very beautiful periods pass in abbreviated time, while periods where not so much happens, or which create a more or less tense expectation about something to come, will be felt as prolonged time. (I will add, in brackets, that this last point is certainly one of the reasons why conductors and musicians often feel like letting a crescendo be accompanied by an accelerando, thereby eliminating the psychological prolongation of time.)

Until now the composer's natural instinct for musical time has told him how the substance must be formed, and how the balance in time and space between all the elements of the music must be. This instinct is still necessary, but one has to underline that comprehension of time as dimension will be of fatal importance for the contemporary composer. He has now a possibility of obtaining a clear and conscious understanding of the dimension of time, just as his colleague nearly four hundred years ago began to get a clear and conscious understanding of the dimension of space, which means of functional harmony.

By virtue of the conditions I have mentioned, creative intelligence and will-power cannot be replaced by, for instance, arithmetical gifts; because creative intelligence can be identified with consciousness about placing the substance in the course of time—an immediate feeling of proportions—while the arithmetical gift is able to work only with symbols on paper, and therefore will either make musical time schematic or give it an inartistic character of casualty or chance.

Finally I want to express the hope that these general remarks about form will create a little more confusion in the picture of tendencies in contemporary music, already quite confused. This is to be understood as a paradox: of course I do not want to make confusion, and I could in the same spirit have expressed the wish that my words might co-operate in eliminating doubt and uncertainty. At the same time, however, I mean that my first wish perhaps might cause you not to feel convinced solely by dialectics but to look for the final reply to this, as to all musical questions, in music itself.

Luciano Berio (ITALY)

I want to consider some problems of our musical life which are facing the conscientious composer who is looking beyond the mere appearance of a musical programme, of a musical institution, or of a public reaction.

These considerations are partially suggested to me by looking at musical programmes during my recent stay in the United States—programmes which have very little to do with our present interests—programmes which suggest too much the idea that music can only be a peaceful and beautiful wonderland, that music is Music, with a capital letter.

No, music is something more. It is made not only with notes. A musical form is first of all an evidence, a testimony—not a mood to be felt, nor a *schema* to be analysed, and not even a fixed system of communication through which men exchange sounds and meanings in the same way in which they exchange merchandise, on the basis of a conventional economic system. This means that first of all as listeners we must ask ourselves why and how a musical work exists, and not just hurriedly if it is right or wrong, beautiful or ugly. Categorical statements, such as right or wrong, beautiful or ugly, typical of the rationalistic thinking of tonal aesthetics, are no longer useful in understanding why and how a composer today works on audible forms and musical action; just as, facing some fundamental problem of life, the idea of good and bad is no longer useful in understanding our reality but represents only a model of moral conventions—conventions, we must remember, that imply in turn the idea of a pre-existing order.

We cannot consider today's music a language, a closed system, precise and comfortable, where everything happens according to prevision, but rather a branch-system of sounds and actions definable and significant only in their actuality and in the relationships which they imply at the moment. Certainly music always tended to formulate itself as a language and even to relate itself to the schemes of spoken language. But this seems today inevitably to degrade music to a code of conventional sensations. The emotional and psychological background tends to overcome and substitute for the scheme of structural relations. Music becomes a catalogue of signals—where, in the worst of cases (forgive the cliché), the trumpet means war, the oboe means a peaceful landscape, the twelve-tone row means anguish, and electronic music represents science fiction. In some aspects, it was the same in the modal language where, as the Pythagorians tell us, the Phrygian mode was used to provoke a fighting spirit and the Hypolydian was used to stimulate sex life. This same thing happens generally in any form of communication, since (we must not forget) information and meaning are not synonymous. The more today's musical language tends to constitute and form itself with reference to a linguistic system, the more it renounces its meaning; and, what is more important, the more predetermined are the relations of the proposed structures, the weaker is the critical conscience of the listeners facing those musical structures.

This is quite a normal process. No matter where or when, this happens if music upholds a magic or ritual function above all. On one hand you have the musician, who, protected by the established powers, or by magic, organizes his effects; and on the other hand, an audience, which wants nothing better than to wallow in these effects. Incidentally, a great part of musical life in concert halls is still based on this kind of ritual, where the interpreter abandons himself to a kind of witchcraft and where the listener, capable of receiving only those code messages of tonal language, seems to find those same guarantees of order and normality which he expects every night, when, in the dark, settling his feet into his slippers, he switches on the television set. The illusion of order and equilibrium is perfect. The listener, the centre of a static, unchangeable universe, finds a confirmation of the general harmony in the legality of a common language, in contemplation of the linguistic order; but he doesn't listen to the form. The "formation of form," as Paul Klee the painter would say, is never taken into consideration, but instead only those artifices of formal suspense—consonance-dissonance, stress-release, expectation-fulfillment—which render the desire for false balance even more acute.

In the face of such situations the composers' and interpreters' responsibility towards the audience, not to speak of the responsibility of the programme makers, becomes obvious, especially if we think, as Henri Pousseur wrote, that it is not possible to explain the sense, the origin, the life of a form without referring to the social relationships from which this form derives, without evoking the relations which it sets up between the individuals who participate in the musical practice in which the form is realized. And this course is not meant to be a persecution of the masterpieces of the system, but rather a case against what the system represents today. The distortions imposed by Mozart and Beethoven on the metric and harmonic formulas, can they not be interpreted as a particular, deliberate way of contributing to change in the world?

During the entire nineteenth century, composers were to refuse more and more to bow to the demands of the public. Their language became always more hermetic. Conscious of what was happening, the public reacted with violence, and the scandalous incidents of *The Rite of Spring* and certain works by Schoenberg represent up to a certain point evident manifestation of awareness by the public. At least up until Webern, all of the works, all of the particular languages of modern music can be explained in these perspectives. When Darius Milhaud in the twenties, for example, superimposed two melodic lines, in themselves very easy, but in two different keys, he manifested in a symbolic way the composer's refusal to act according to a required *schema*.

Today the effects of the revolution are evident. The literal reconstruction of the drama of the sonata form, which gave us so many classical masterpieces, leaves an impression of family theatricals. The audience, which is carried away by the events of that drama, knowing from the very beginning that it will have a happy ending on a tonic chord, could very easily represent a society fundamentally orientated towards acquisition of a swimming pool.

Today the composers refuse to continue representing what they justly consider to be an hypocrisy. The musical revolution of these last fifty years, confirmed by analogous experiences in the literary and painting fields, has educated us to evaluate the musical experience no longer as a predisposed *schema*, but a direct place where are formed, created and developed the elements of communication—that are never *ready*-made, but have always to *be* made. Briefly, the chosen material and the form become as one. To put it very simply, music can no longer be transcribed for piano, for instance; it is no longer transposable as the tonal schemes had been; but will be one unit with its concrete actuality.

On this very general principle are based the structural processes in today's music, which imply the possibility of inventing each time a structural *schema*, according to the nature of the chosen material—and this gives the composers the possibility and the need of exploring new fields of sound-production—electronic music, for instance, is the most discussed today. A common ground of development, still attached to the quality of the sound material, between electronic music and performed music, is that both today can be characterized by the same stylistic tendency, by the same aesthetic principle, mainly developed upon the unifying powers of the serial system. I am referring to the fact that a great amount of liberty is given to the performer.

For a long time European music did not give such liberty to the performer—that is, since the time when the part of the *basso continuo* was realized extemporarily at the harpsichord. Especially in instrumental music, there are now many works in which the performer is no longer a means, an intermediary, but a collaborator. He is given a plan of action, more or less precise, a certain number of structures which he can arrange in the way most congenial to himself. The composition again in this case is no longer something ready-made, but rather to be made, made to fit. From a means of communication, it becomes a means of co-operation, and this kind of open form has sometimes rendered necessary new concepts of notation which would no longer be based exclusively on quantities but rather on qualities, not only on notes but also on actions.

All this ties in directly with the poetics of the *opera aperta* (open form), or, as it is called in English, "work in progress," which has existed for a long time in the fields of painting, literature, and the theatre. At a minimum level, open form means all those objects, often not essential, and almost always very costly, with which we would like to fill our homes, which range from hinged lamps, sectional libraries in various styles, or chairs capable of metamorphosis, to the mobiles by Calder and others. On a broader level an *opera aperta* can be the University of Caracas, designed as a school which is invented each day. The rooms of this school are made of sliding walls, in such a way that teachers and pupils, according to the humanistic and architectural problem at hand, can construct a suitable study atmosphere, continually modifying the internal structure of the building. In jazz, a notable example of open form is the jam session, during which, on the basis of a given theme and harmonic scheme, and on the basis of a repertoire of common stylistic conventions and inventions, the performers build the musical object in a remarkably unpredictable way and obtain a performance which is never equal to any preceding one.

In the field of literature, the phenomenon reveals vaster and deeper roots. It is sufficient only to name James Joyce, Mallarmé, Proust (in a certain sense), e e cummings, Bertolt Brecht, and Kafka. And perhaps it is almost superfluous to recall Mallarmé's *Le Livre*, which has actually inspired one of the most interesting piano compositions of the new music, the Third Piano Sonata by Pierre Boulez. And the same thing applies to James Joyce's works, *Ulysses*, and still more *Finnegans Wake*. Here really the text opens up to a series of always-new readings, because there is such a complex richness of relationships that the reader gives a new interpretation at each new reading, discovering not only links of allusions, but also a concrete reality that is continually changing.

This openness does not occur only on this plane. If we look at the theatrical poetics of Bertolt Brecht, we find a concept of dramatic action which does not want the spectator to believe, but wants to present the facts in a detached way—in fact the Brechtian drama in its strictest expression does not elaborate any solution. It is up to the spectator to make his own critical conclusions from what he has seen, even if that places him in an ambiguous situation; the work is open just as a debate is open; the solution is awaited and desired, but must occur with the conscious assistance of the audience. The work in progress becomes an instrument of education in self-direction for contemporary men.

To a certain extent the same thing happens also in music, where the composer furnishes the interpreter with starting-points, with general lines of action, with proposals and suggestions to which the performer must react in a constantly renewed way. And in order for this to happen it must be very carefully planned, of course, in terms of musical composition. I should say that the more freedom that is given to the interpreter, and to the audience of course, the more the structure of the composition becomes complex and the more difficult is the composer's task. He must prevent chaos from destroying all the possible relationships. The most important procedure is to give a certain degree of redundancy to the texture that constitutes a kind of buffer state between chaos and the fields of possible meanings. (An analysis of Boulez's *Improvisation sur Mallarmé* would be in this case very useful.) But when the buffer state is not established, when the tendency to give freedom to the interpreter is pushed to its limit, the composer is evidently condemned to renounce ever making free decisions—to no longer giving any signs for any interpretation whatsoever.

But finally nothing prevents us from always asking of music a certain system of probability—a *style*, I would say—a bridge between a renewed material and the renewed conception of form, a bridge that helps us to transcend, continuously, always, all the ideas that we have about the world and about ourselves. It is through artistic creation in fact that we hope to approach, without ever reaching, the essence of everything.

Discussion

Jean Papineau-Couture (CANADA): Mr Berio is probably the last person in the world to be thought of as a traditionalist or an academic. However, in listening to him speak, I said to myself, as I have indeed done several times during this conference, that the romantic age is truly far from ended. What characterizes the romantic age, in my opinion, is precisely the fact that, continually, musical decisions are made for non-musical reasons. I observed here all the citations from literature; the *opera aperta* is to be thought of as reminiscent of modern "slice-of-life" fiction; literature is to serve as a model for music. Now, the "slice-of-life" novel, which is pretty well dead in literature today, certainly cannot serve as a model for music—because there's nothing musical about it.

Music is an object complete in itself, whatever style it may be written in. If I make music, my reasons should be musical. If I make a painting, my reasons should be those of the art of painting. The same holds for all the arts. But at present our reasons tend to be non-musical—and it was the romantics, Berlioz and others, who started this attitude.

Let's remember that the chief musical reason, the sole reason that is essentially musical is this: Can the listener, receiving the auditory signal produced in music, that is, the sound (whatever it may be), can he make out of it any kind of *construction*? Only starting from that point, and not by making descriptions and "programmes" or going to the score to see what is written, can a listener be persuaded that a work is worth while—not worth while just as novelty (that is of no importance), but worth while in itself.

I don't want you to think I'm speaking as a reactionary. It's quite evident that if the composer has not the impression that he is doing something new, and that he belongs to his time, he won't ever create anything vital. But this means that it's necessary for him to concern himself with this fact: that an intelligent listener, blessed with a good pair of ears, can make a unity out of his sounds. If he hasn't done that, he simply hasn't made a work of musical art.

Berio: I think there's a misunderstanding there about the "slice-of-life" novel. I wasn't speaking of that, in any case. Proust, Joyce, cummings—they are quite a different case from that. Anyway, I made these references from outside the orbit of music partly to avoid a prolonged discussion of technical points before a mixed audience such as this. You were completely authentic in your reaction. It belongs to the French aesthetic, and has for about one hundred and twenty years. Your cultural view is very French. It is to detach music from life, in a sense. But basically music has a real, a concrete function in the human community—always—even John Cage—as well as Verdi. This is the main point. I think that attitude towards music was responsible, for twenty or thirty years, for the most bitter misunderstanding of Debussy's music, for instance—one of the greatest composers—which was always taken as a kind of *musique d'ameublement* or afternoon-tea music. Through a new quality of approach to music, such a great master has been re-evaluated. Perhaps we should try to define romanticism. I believe romanticism is still a component of men today.

Papineau-Couture: You want to distinguish between romanticism and lyricism.

Berio: You were talking about romanticism.

Papineau-Couture: Yes, but I think *you* are talking about lyricism.

Jan Matějcek (CZECHOSLOVAKIA): Did Mr Berio in his paper mention that the conception of good and evil is relegated to an area of convention? Did I understand him correctly?

Berio: Music is a testimony, in any time, of *men*. First of all, faced with a musical work, personally, I prefer to react in this way: to see *why* it exists and what's *beyond* that. The aesthetic and the catalogue of feelings (such as good and bad) come much later; I even think it's to a certain extent uninteresting.

Matějček: Don't you feel that music should nevertheless try to express feeling?

Berio: The word "feeling" in English is one of the most ambiguous, the most open to meanings. Feelings can be—anything. Of course feeling enters the picture. Human perception cannot be divided. We are—as men we are a *Gestalt*, a sum.

Part Three
Summary

CONFERENCE SUMMARY

Marvin Duchow (CANADA)

We have at last come to the close of this incredible week of intense, often informative, and always stimulating deliberations and encounters. If we could now, for but a brief moment, regain our equipoise after these exhilarating, if vertiginous, shifts from the fantastic realm of electronic sound to the earthbound intricacies of musical copyright,[1] or from the metaphysical profundities of psychological time to the reverberating rhythms of improvised jazz, or yet again from the steely rigidities of total serialism to the unnerving fluidities of musical indeterminacy, then we might, I think, be in a position to cast a sober backward glance over the week's proceedings, and to attempt a provisional assessment.

We have during this past week concerned ourselves with certain crucial problems of the contemporary composer first in relation to his audience, secondly in relation to his intermediary, the performer, and thirdly with respect to his own craft.

It is the first of these relationships, and the crucial problem of the widening gap between the contemporary composer and his audience, which remains for me one of the areas least decisively penetrated. If I remind you, however, that this is probably the most fundamental, as well as one of the most complex and elusive, of the problems confronting the contemporary composer—one for which

[1] During the Composers' Conference, a discussion on "Composers' rights" and international copyright law took place, chaired by W. St. Clair Low of the Composers Authors and Publishers Association of Canada, with Klaus Egge of Norway and Guy Warrack of Great Britain as participating composers.

the discussion of mere musical styles and techniques conducted *ad nauseam* can provide no real solution—then we can, I think, more readily appreciate the difficulty of the task undertaken by the members of that particular panel. Symptoms of the widening gap were, of course, noted and facts cited, as when Mr Legley spoke of the virtual disappearance of a chamber music audience in Belgium. Mr Legley's constructive suggestion that amateur chamber-music playing be encouraged and cultivated as a means of creating an audience for this medium might well be noted. Indirectly related to this point was Mr Adaskin's very practical suggestion, at a later session, that composers concern themselves increasingly with the writing of early graded material in contemporary idioms for the training of students and amateurs. Being myself an educator, I heartily concur in these suggestions, and am certain that, properly implemented, their at least partially remedial effect would soon be felt. It will become evident, however, during the subsequent course of my address why I cannot consider such remedial measures truly pertinent to the central problems confronting the artist in our day.

It will be recalled that the eminently practical discussions of problems arising from the composer's relationship to the performer yielded a number of quite specific recommendations for the simplification of technique and of rhythmic notation. The illusion of limitless technical resource seems to have created in the mind of many a contemporary composer an obsessive disregard for the performer. Mr Schuller's and Mr Feldbrill's memorable pleas on behalf of that long-suffering individual seemed timely and well taken. While time did not permit of more than a very fragmentary discussion of the problems of rhythmic notation, a worth-while suggestion did emerge in the form of Mr Papineau-Couture's proposal that a body be set up to study a possible revision of our notational system—a suggestion surely meriting careful consideration.

I turn lastly to the problems of the composer in relation to his craft, as discussed during this past week. A comprehensive spectrum of opinion and of artistic belief has been in evidence here, ranging all the way from several carefully thought-out statements of deep-rooted and healthy conservatism, through various shades of more radical opinion, to the most advanced degrees of experimentalism—all most cogently and clearly expressed. It is perhaps the physical concurrence of so heterogeneous a group of distinguished musicians ready to discuss in open forum the underlying assumptions and principles of their artistic creeds which marks this conference as different from the more partisan festivals of contemporary music in Europe, and which would lead at least one participant to hope that it might become a recurrent event.

Serialism expectedly dominated the scene during much of these discussions. I, for one, was grateful for the moderate and sober statements of Mr. Iain Hamilton on this subject which, while noting the exhaustion of traditional tonal means, affirmed the present need to reconstitute the elements of music (melody, texture, density, rhythm, and so on), and to discover forms that would be valid in terms of these reconstituted elements. Mr Hamilton's cautionary remarks concerning the irrelevance of technical formulations in the appreciation of a musical work were admirably stated, and found many echoes in the comments of other speakers.

From Mr Krenek's paper we learned about the *dernier cri* in compositional fashions—namely, randomness, or indeterminacy, as the prevailing slogans have it. According to the proponents of this astonishing, and rather terrifying doctrine, the musical work—or any entity in our physical world, for that matter—is regarded as the mere sport of chance, no more inevitable or justifiable in its autonomy of form than any other conceivable agglomeration of components. Clearly, the rigid determinism of total serialism is here rejected. In fact, for these musicians, as Mr Krenek has reported, "the era of the twelve-tone technique is over, in fact, such a thing as twelve-tone composition never existed." Mr Krenek's own relatively moderate position apparently aims at achieving random effects through arithmetical manipulations of the series.

Equally preoccupied with the dilemma of total serialism versus randomness, Mr George Rochberg suggested in his thoughtful and provocative paper that, paradoxically, each of these polar alternatives creates an identical effect in desiccating the flow of time, thus destroying the possibility of formal integration within the work. This conclusion was based upon an elaborate psychological hypothesis that warrants careful study.

A more colourful rival claimed our attention during the closing sessions of this conference in the lively debate on electronic music. Whatever may be our individual opinions on this controversial subject, we are all, I believe, most grateful for the opportunity of hearing these relatively inaccessible, and provocative works. For those who are professionally interested in the field, the reports of Mr Tal and Mr Ussachevsky, and the enlightening comments of Dr LeCaine, Mr Berio, Mr Badings, and others on this subject must surely have proven instructive.

So much, then, by way of sketchy review and summary of the events of this past week. There are, needless to say, many important points which I have necessarily omitted owing to lack of time. There is, however, one issue which—although it has not appeared explicitly in any discussion—has been implicit in some. I think here of Mr Blomdahl's account of the poetic content of his opera *Aniara* as well as certain other reports. Since I consider the matter in question vitally relevant to, though not explicit in, our deliberations, I shall take the liberty of elaborating upon it.

Perhaps the simplest way to introduce the subject with which I am here concerned is to refer to a current definition of the term "meaning." Semanticists define the concept in terms of a triadic— or triangular—relationship involving three points of reference: (*a*) the observer of the meaningful event, (*b*) the event designated by him as meaningful, and (*c*) the datum to which that event is held to refer.

Considering the meaningfulness, or significance, of music, we note that in Greek antiquity two concepts existed. One related the art to a metaphysical ordering of the universe; the other—the Platonic tradition—discovered in it both a reflection of human personality conceived in ideal categories and, concomitantly, an instrument for the development of character. Thus, an enriching duality of meaning was claimed for the art in that its significance was held to reside in both human and extra-human, or divine, values. It must be understood, of course, that, as with all meaning, these significations are imputed—are ascribed—and are not in any sense absolutely inherent. It is, however, just such structures of collectively imputed meanings that constitute the fabric of a culture.

The rich and elevating interplay of meanings ascribed to music as a phenomenon persisted during the era of mediaeval Christianity which witnessed the formulation of new theoretical classifications again dividing music into categories of divine, human, terrestrial, and so forth. The organic system of interrelations between these categories as articulated in mediaeval philosophy underlay and, in fact, made possible, the pregnant meaningfulness which the Gregorian Chant as a liturgical form held for the men of that age, but which it has lost for us, retaining little more than its aesthetic meaning, that is, the intrinsic relationships arising from the interplay of its musical parts—a not inconsiderable content, but a transformed and surely a devaluated one nonetheless.

It is important to understand too, in this connection, that both the rational complexity and the affective significance of the idea to be represented, or symbolized—in this instance, the conceptual order of the mediaeval universe—place their stamp upon, and determine the form of, the symbol itself. Here, the triadic relationship inherent in the concept of meaning becomes operative. Thus, we begin with a felt impulse on the part of (*a*) the sentient observer of the meaningful event to create (*b*) a symbol that will serve as the adequate referent for, or counterpart of (*c*) the datum observed or conceptualized. Let me demonstrate this point in a somewhat different way that may perhaps have some bearing on contemporary notions of randomness, however well founded these appear to be in current scientific theory. It has been pointed out statistically that, if enough monkeys were to play upon enough typewriters for a long enough time, eventually one of them would be bound to hammer out the text of, let us say, one of Shakespeare's plays. But, even if this were to happen, it is important for us to realize that this would only be a travesty, a trick of chance, and not a meaningful event, since the triadic relationship involving both volition and reference is absent. Some may, of course, prefer to reduce art to a mere random phenomenon. There remains, however, the more truly human alternative which conceives it to be a purposive and significant endeavour.

Let us return, however, to our historical *précis*. That abundant interplay of meanings ascribed to music during the Middle Ages gradually broke down during the Renaissance and Baroque, during which periods transposed modes of artistic meaning and evaluation were evolved. Thus, in Elizabethan times, a simple pavane and galliard possessed a certain dimension of meaning whereby they were envisaged metaphorically (that is, more in a playful literary, rather than in a truly metaphysical sense) as reflecting the motion of the celestial spheres. The tradition of the German Baroque remains, on the other hand, in a sense more directly linked with mediaeval values. In marvelling at the supreme musical works of the German Baroque from Scheidt to J. S. Bach, we tend to forget that the intensity and grandeur of that style derive from the very fact that skill of craft and artistic excellence were not considered to be self-sufficient ends, but were held to be preconditions for other goals. It was again the symbolic act of envisaging the complexity of this art as a fitting tribute to, and a worthy token of, the Deity that shaped the work and gave it its essential character.

If from the term "divine" we exclude the association of divinity—a truly radical emendation—retaining solely its connection of the extra-human, we are left with the basis for those rationalist and scientific doctrines that were engendered during the Renaissance, and that form so characteristic a part of the intellectual and conceptual climate of modernity. This again yields a duality of meanings ascribable to music—a duality different from, let us say, that of Greek times in that these meanings are no longer interrelated, but are now disparate and mutually exclusive. Thus, on the one hand, music may still be understood in some way to symbolize aspects of human experience. That experience may be understood in a collective sense, as appears to be in some degree the position of certain of our panelists, such as, for instance, Mr Legley (if I appraise correctly his position), and the Soviet delegate—although each in quite different interpretations of that premise. More typically, however, it is a highly individualized experience that is here embodied, as in the tradition of the Impressionists, or of our latter-day hedonists, for whom musical value resides solely in the quality and variety of sensuous experience that can be elicited by shifting patterns of sonority. The formalist, on the other hand, invests the musical work with no referential signification. Its meaning, for him—if, indeed, he concedes that it has any meaning at all—is purely intrinsic, and will be understood as perhaps an organic, a mechanistic, or even a chance arrangement of its elements, whose only significance is held to lie within the actual pattern of their interrelationships. In other words, the work is held in this view to possess an autonomy and an objective validity that completely removes it from the world of subjective experience.

Despite the evident oversimplification of my presentation, many will, I think, discern in the disparity and antagonism of meanings outlined in the foregoing an impoverishment in relation to the more integrated concepts of earlier periods. The solipsist position implicit in the presence of mutually exclusive doctrines, and more particularly within the hedonistic attitude as such, seems, however, inescapable in our culture, and must be taken as a measure of the tragic position of the artist in modern times.

I should like to quote a brief passage from an unpublished paper on an older composer not in our midst—Paul Hindemith—who has chosen not to follow the byways of experimentalism, but has chosen rather (in, for instance, such works as the opera *Mathis der Maler*) to face this greater issue: "... unlike most contemporary composers, Hindemith has been concerned with the problem of restoring to the art of music that significance which it formerly possessed through having been subsumed under a system of either religious or metaphysical values, and which it has since lost. Perhaps no less important in this connection than the revival of ancient metaphysical doctrines is the ethical bias which has apparently played an important role in shaping Hindemith's artistic development and which provides a further clue to the order of his symbolic thought...."

It is not, however, upon quite this note that I should like to close. The recent experiments in, and exploration of, new musical resources are too vital, too potentially rich and fertile to be disregarded—just as, however, the ethical and artistic confrontations of the contemporary composer are issues too profound to be bypassed. If the lessons of history have aught to teach us in these matters, we may hope that a Monteverdi will, in the not too remote future, appear upon the scene to master the elements of the new musical language that appears to be emerging, and to invest these too often idle counters with symbolic content and with a deeper signification. There are, I would venture to say, some portents in evidence at this historic Conference that that day may not be too distantly remote.

Discussion

Elizabeth Maconchy (GREAT BRITAIN): Little has been said [during the Conference] about the future direction which serial music is likely to take. Total serialism may be the right way in the view of some composers, but others feel that this strait jacket is restricting to the point of immobility. Will the strait jacket burst at the seams? And in what direction? One of the most frequent criticisms of serial technique is that it must (anyway to some extent) inhibit spontaneity. It seems that many composers now feel the need of a greater degree of spontaneity in their work, and so the performer is given freedom of choice—as to the order in which he will play certain sections of a work, for instance, or in some cases he is instructed to extemporize, and so on. But why does the composer wish to surrender to the performer the spontaneity which is surely the composer's own birthright? I only suggest these questions in the hope that there may be time to talk about them, and about other points connected with the actual process of composition, for which we have had too little time up till now. I would greatly like to hear more from Mr Gunther Schuller, for instance, whose paper on jazz was full of the most interesting and stimulating ideas.

Another point: it has been very valuable to have heard a number of electronic works, and to get some idea of the very different approaches that are being made to electronic composition by the various composers represented here. I can only speak very tentatively and hesitantly about this, but after listening to the works we have heard it seems to me that electronic composers will now above all be concerned with further defining or formulating their medium in order further to subject it to the discipline which is an essential to the making of any work of art. In some works, for instance perhaps the two Italian works by Maderna and Berio, one could apprehend a form, which one was not so much aware of in some of the other examples. These are only tentative suggestions, however.

Sir Ernest MacMillan (CANADA): I came here somewhat like the solitary lion in a den of Daniels—that is to say, in a receptive mood!—and I have been in no way disappointed. There has been a great deal of food for thought; but I would rather allow, after Dr Duchow's admirable summary (I think he has covered practically the whole ground), that other members of the audience express themselves. I am filled with admiration for the organization, for the Canadian League of Composers, and particularly for those on whom the chief burden [of organizing the Conference] has fallen; we might mention Mr Applebaum first: this was his brain-child; I was very sceptical about it myself at first, but I'm certainly convinced that it has been (in the words of *1066 And All That*) a Good Thing. Also we must not forget our president, Mr Weinzweig, and Mr Kasemets, the conference secretary.

John Beckwith (CANADA): There have been so many loose ends—Miss Maconchy suggested this, with restraint I think—many, many loose ends left, sometimes out of the unavoidable scheduling arrangements which did not allow enough time for discussion. I have listed just a few points which we might remind ourselves of, in the realm of "unfinished business."

There's the point which Miss Maconchy touched on, namely: Mr Schuller presented a paper which brought up the question of jazz in its relation to contemporary musical techniques, and very provocatively I must say. Personally I found it not convincing, because in the whole area of relating jazz to contemporary musical creation nobody has made the definitions clear. Mr Schuller was only able to do it by playing us a record of what was *not* in his opinion jazz, followed by a record of what *was* in his opinion jazz. Now I believe this is a fertile field; Mr Schuller's own compositions, which excite me very much, show that this is a fertile field. We have not, sad to say, had time to discuss it, particularly with him present.

Then in the session on "Performer Versus Composer" (I use the term "versus"), the composers were read a little lecture on how they must be tidy, and how they must take the performer into account, the fact that he has five fingers and not eight on each hand and so on. On the other hand, nobody among us timid composers was bold enough to stand up and shake a finger at the performer (not at those who were present, by the way, because there are exceptions) but at the majority of performers who, as Mr Schuller mentioned parenthetically, are lazy, and do not practise new music to a nearly sufficient degree.

A word came up in Mr Blomdahl's paper which sent shivers down many spines, I'm quite sure. That word was "entertainment." Nobody tossed that word around; and perhaps it should have been tossed around a bit. Is the composer merely abdicating his integrity when he considers the use of music—in association with stage, for example, and in association with some forms of literature, and so on—as directed to a broad public which seeks in musical manifestations some quality of entertainment? That question was a loose end; that word—it should have been a rather electric one.

Again, an exchange, Mr Luening called it a duet, between Mr Blomdahl and Mr Berio, presented the unsolved dilemma of whether one really has the same thing when one has a tone blown by human wind through a French horn and when one produces a

French-horn tone with a synthesizer. Mr LeCaine, I think very rightly, jumped on that as an extremely important dilemma to discuss; is it the sound of a humanly blown French horn which you prefer, or is it merely what you are doing with the sound? That, too, had to be left up in the air.

We had in the person of Mr Berio, I believe, the only panelist of the week who has had some experience with the attempt to make a musical form through co-operation of performer and composer, and we should perhaps question Mr Berio as to how he feels this works. As a provoking thought on this question I would only mention an experience which was relayed to me about the performance of one of these pieces, I believe it was a piece by Stockhausen written in this fashion, where there are a group of sections of a work which the performer will play in any order which appeals to him. The experience was this: the performer (who was going to give this, by the way, in a concert) *practised it*. This perhaps shouldn't happen; but this performer practised it, found that there was a particular order which pleased him and played that order, having practised it in that order. And I'm told that the composer objected very strenuously to this.

Mr Berio replied to the last statement by quoting his experiences with a solo flute work, Sequenza, *which by its flexible adaptation to the personal qualities of a performer had encouraged him to pursue this creative approach further. In reply to another question he quoted Paul Valéry's remark that "two dangers hang over the world—order and disorder"; and said he felt it was impossible at present to lay down a syntax or series of theoretical or pedagogical formulas for the new indeterminate forms.*

Eugene Kash (CANADA): It has almost been taken for granted at this week's Conference that we have outgrown even twelve-tone music, that it's a dead thing. But you, Dr Duchow, in your position at McGill, and other educators have a tremendous task of getting your teachers to change their attitude on repertoire. The composers have to start talking to teachers rather than to each other.

Michael Olver (CANADA): Vocal music has been touched on in some aspects, but not the relationship between the composer and the singer. In instrumental technique the problems have always been the same. There has never been a time when there hasn't been an instrumentalist who said to his contemporary, the composer: "I can't possibly play that!"—but there is always a possibility that somehow or other technique may be developed to the point where such a passage *can* be mastered. But with the voice, I feel, the question is a little more intense. Here you are dealing with a musical intellect directly, not merely with what your ten fingers can do. The singer has to conceive the musical idea right here inside his head and express it with his voice.

Duchow: On the point of the difficulty of contemporary vocal music, it struck me as you spoke, Mr Olver, that some of the works we heard yesterday seem to have surmounted those difficulties very well. [The Conference concert devoted to electronic music included some works with "live" vocal portions.]

Murray Adaskin (CANADA): Perhaps this might help to answer this question partially. Thirty-odd years ago, Paul Hindemith wrote the song cycle *Das Marienleben*; and he rewrote the work—some of the songs as many as twenty-five times—and he said that his earlier experiences with singers made him feel that he would be just willing to wait, as Schoenberg is said to have done with the sixth finger. But he finally came to the conclusion that it was really his fault, and he found that he could rewrite the work still retaining what he wanted to say and yet making it possible for the human voice to handle.

Cathy Berberian (ITALY): I have felt, as a singer, that many people have exaggerated the problems of contemporary music for singers. I've often been told, "Oh, but you'll ruin your voice!" and "Don't you do any other kind of singing? I'm sure you can't ever do anything that's fluid and *bel canto*." Well, all singers have to study vocal production; otherwise the voice doesn't come out; it stays inside. That is supposedly *bel canto*, but actually all it is is placing the voice, learning how to produce the tones correctly. Once you have learned how to produce these tones correctly, no matter where you sing, no matter what part of your scale you are singing, it is always correct; even if it is a question of a thirteenth of an interval, that doesn't change the fact that the placement of the tone is correct. I find that I do contemporary music and go back to traditional classical music and the classical music gains a great deal by what I've done with the contemporary music; and it's a similar thing going back again to contemporary music after I've done some classical. They help each other. The difficulties are surmounted only by the fact that if you hear enough of contemporary music as a singer (as every instrumentalist should do when he's going to face performing contemporary music), you become used to it; you understand what you are facing, and it doesn't become such a bug-a-boo as it would if you had only known Rossini and Donizetti and Debussy.

THE CONCERTS OF THE CONFERENCE

Udo Kasemets

Musical Programmes Presented during the International Conference of Composers

I

National Festival Orchestra and Wind Ensemble
Victor Feldbrill
Frederick Prausnitz
conductors

Fugue for string orchestra	KARL HÖLLER
Sonata for chamber orchestra	IAIN HAMILTON
Pièce concertante no. 1 for piano and strings	JEAN PAPINEAU-COUTURE
Mario Bernardi, piano	
Deserts, for winds, percussion, and tapes	EDGARD VARÈSE
Chamber Concerto for piano, wind, and percussion	KARL-BIRGER BLOMDAHL
William Aide, piano	

II

Chamber Music

Music for clarinet, trumpet, and viola, Op. 27	KARL SCHISKE

Stanley McCartney, clarinet; Joseph Umbrico, trumpet; Stephen Kondaks, viola

Drei Zigeunerromanzen	HERMANN REUTTER

Mary Simmons, soprano; the composer at the piano

Nonet	OTTO JOACHIM

Mildred Goodman, violin; Stephen Kondaks, viola; Malcolm Tait, cello; Paul Olynik, bass; Dirk Keetbaas, flute; Stanley McCartney, clarinet; Eugene Rittich, horn; Norman Tobias, bassoon; Mario Bernardi, piano

Sechs Vermessene	ERNST KRENEK

the composer at the piano

Duo Concertante   GEORGE ROCHBERG
Hyman Goodman, violin; Donald Whitton, cello
Septet (1953)   IGOR STRAVINSKY
*Morry Kernerman, violin; Stanley Solomon, viola; Isaac Mammot, cello;
Stanley McCartney, clarinet; Eugene Rittich, horn;
Norman Tobias, bassoon; Mario Bernardi, piano*

III
Electronic Music

Capriccio for violin with electronic accompaniment	HENK BADINGS
Genese (music for five sine-wave generators)	HENK BADINGS
Study in Sound	VLADIMIR USSACHEVSKY
Suite from *King Lear*	VLADIMIR USSACHEVSKY AND OTTO LUENING
Invenzione su una voce	BRUNO MADERNA
Thema (Omaggio a James Joyce)	LUCIANO BERIO
Aria for mezzo-soprano with Fontana Mix	JOHN CAGE

Cathy Berberian, mezzo-soprano

IV
Orchestra of the International String Congress

Roy Harris
conductor

Hymn and Fuguing Tune no. 1	HENRY COWELL
Tableau	HARRY FREEDMAN
Two Etudes	GODFREY RIDOUT
Rapsodia Elegiaca	HECTOR CAMPOS-PARSI
Adios a Villa-Lobos	JUAN JOSE CASTRO
Bachianas Brasilieras no. 5	HEITOR VILLA-LOBOS

Maria Esther Robles, soprano

Passacaglia, Cadenza, and Fugue, for piano and strings   ROY HARRIS
Johana Harris, piano

V
Canadian Broadcasting Corporation Symphony Orchestra

Walter Susskind
conductor

Symphonic poem, "Mtsyri"   OTAR TAKTAKISHVILI
the composer conducting
Symphony   ISTVÁN ANHALT
Wine of Peace, two songs for soprano and orchestra   JOHN WEINZWEIG
Mary Simmons, soprano
Les Offrandes oubliées (méditation symphonique)   OLIVIER MESSIAEN
Music for Orchestra, Op. 50   WALLINGFORD RIEGGER

Though the presentations of prepared papers, the ensuing panel discussions and the question-answer periods from the floor provided considerable insight into the working methods, artistic philosophy, aesthetic convictions, and technical manipulations of the participating composers of the Conference, the aim of the meeting would have remained without fulfilment if these verbal encounters had not been complemented by presentations of live music. It was for this purpose that the programme of the Conference included five concerts, devoted mainly to works by participating composers.

Technical and financial considerations did not permit the inclusion of music by all (almost three score) delegates of the Conference, yet an attempt was made to build a programme which would give fair geographical and stylistic representation of the participating composers. All told, thirty works by twenty-nine composers were performed. Of those, nine works belonged to composers who were not in attendance at the Conference: Villa-Lobos' *Bachianas Brasilieras no. 5* was played in memoriam of the deceased master; Riegger's *Music for Orchestra* was scheduled as a commemoration of the composer's seventy-fifth birthday; Stravinsky's, Cage's, and Maderna's works were included as characteristic examples of present-day stylistic trends; Messiaen had to cancel his participation at the Conference at the last moment; three compositions by non-participating Western-Hemisphere composers were presented by the visiting Orchestra of the International String Congress, the leader of which, Roy Harris, compiled the programme independently of the Conference Programme Committee.

Since the concert of the last-mentioned orchestra was entirely devoted to music from the Americas (featuring works by two United States, two Canadian, and three Latin-American composers), at first sight the regional representation of composers may seem lopsided in favour of this continent: nineteen Americans vs. ten Europeans. Yet discounting this special event, the balance for the remaining concerts shows a much fairer picture: twelve Americans vs. ten Europeans. When one considers that half of this dozen of residents of the American continent are native Europeans, thus having direct ties with both cultures, the regional representation of composers must be considered almost ideal.

Similar care was exercised in planning the programmes with regard to their musical content. Though, owing to their actuality, serial music and music conceived by synthetic means had become the most prominent topics during the discussions, in concert programmes fair share was given to works representing the "other side." Of thirty compositions played during the Conference, eleven were based on non-serial principles and the same number were founded on serial manipulations in one form or another. Seven electronic works, presented in a special programme, and one combining wind and percussion sounds with *musique concrète* on tape, rounded out the figures to provide a representative cross-section of present-day compositional trends.

Though the five concerts fell in distinct categories—chamber orchestra, chamber music, electronic music, string orchestra, symphony orchestra—the forms and media chosen by the composers were of the greatest variety. Besides five purely orchestral works and six compositions for strings alone, there were three concertante works for piano and orchestra, three compositions combining voice with instruments, two combining voice with magnetic tapes, two employing both instruments and tapes, in addition to five purely electronic compositions and four chamber or solo works.

This abundant variety provided the attending delegates, participating musicians, and visiting public (whose numbers were often beyond most optimistic expectations) with a feast of contemporary music previously unknown in the annals of Canadian music. For the Conference participants the compositions presented were a springboard for further discussions which were frequently carried into late night hours and often led into more music listening via phonograph and magnetic tape. For Canadian performers the week meant hard work in media which are not overly practised during the regular concert season. Be it said here that our local musicians met the often enormous demands of the scores with enthusiasm, skill, intelligence, and highly commendable musicianship. The public and critics had an opportunity to get acquainted with music of our time in a large package and had in addition a chance to evaluate the place of Canadian music on the international scene. That the works by Anhalt, Freedman, Joachim, Papineau-Couture, Ridout, and Weinzweig were able to hold their own in their prominent company only proves that in the post-war years Canada has taken great strides in creative music and now can unhesitatingly assume a place among the countries which make serious contributions to the art of musical composition.

Speaking of individual works in the programme, the place of honour belongs undoubtedly to Edgard Varèse's *Deserts* for winds, percussion, and magnetic tapes. In this score, composed from 1952 to 1954, the ever-young seventy-five-year-old innovator from New York juxtaposes the sounds of fourteen woodwinds and brasses in addition to a battery of percussive instruments with what he calls "organized sounds," produced by means of magnetic tapes over two stereophonic loudspeakers. By turns subtle, violent, energetic, and dense, the music moves from one surprise to another and leaves any listener, sympathetic or hostile, under its gripping impact. Here a master sets an example of artistic honesty, vital imagination, and musical intuition—a combination only too rarely found or seldom uncompromisingly cultivated among creative musicians.

Though none of the other works performed during the Conference reached the towering heights of the *Deserts*, there were many which demonstrated their creators' sincerity, inquisitive mind, and keen musical ear. There were experiments where only the composers themselves know how much they succeeded in solving their posed problems. There were works following traditional patterns which established quick contact with the listeners. To weigh their merits against each other would be useless and impossible. One can only speak in terms of individual approaches toward the art of composition, a phenomenon of which the Conference was a showcase.

Of the experimental works next to Varèse's *Deserts*, only one other juxtaposed instrumental sounds with magnetophonically reproduced sounds: Otto Joachim's *Nonet*. Here the tape recorder is used to play the reversion of the opening movement of the work as its finale. The middle section, consisting of five variations and scored for four instruments, brings in the chance element by leaving the order of the variations to the individual player's discretion.

Recorded violin sound combined with electronically conceived sounds forms the basis of Dutch composer Henk Badings' *Capriccio*. Here, as well as in his *Genese* (music for five sine-wave generators), the composer attempts to find a synthesis of electronic devices and traditional form-patterns.

Much farther off in experimental direction are the montages of human voice and electronic sounds by the two Italians, Luciano Berio and Bruno Maderna, and the *enfant terrible* of American music, John Cage. In the latter's *Aria for mezzo-soprano with Fontana Mix* the composer creates a surrealistic picture assigning to the vocal soloist hisses, barks, declamations, straight singing lines, and coloratura passages of the greatest variety and linguistic Babel. Maderna in turn provides the singer in his *Invenzione su una voce* with a vocal line which simultaneously runs in distorted form as the magnetophonic background. Berio's work dispenses with the live performer altogether, save for reading an excerpt from Joyce's *Ulysses* as an introduction to his *Thema (Omaggio a James Joyce)*. The composition itself consists of electronically manipulated syllables and sounds of the presented text.

Among the experimental music one has to list Vladimir Ussachevsky's *Study in Sound* and the same composer's joint opus with Otto Luening, a suite from their incidental music to *King Lear*—both already established classics in their medium.

The remainder of the programme shied away from experiment in its extreme sense. Search for new forms or novel instrumental sound-combinations remained here the main preoccupation of most composers, whereas a minority attempted to find musical expression by well-established means.

Of the latter, Soviet composer Otar Taktakishvili's symphonic poem *Mtsyri* has to be mentioned in the first place. A romantic piece of outright programme music it follows the nationalistic Russian tradition of Rimsky-Korsakov and Borodin.

Germany's Karl Höller's *Fugue for String Orchestra* is based on solid classical tradition tinged with unobtrusive chromaticism and his compatriot Hermann Reutter's *Drei Zigeunerromanzen* look back towards the German Lied and Italian recitative for their inspiration. Classical objectivity and folkloristic romanticism were also the main characteristics of the programme offered by the International String Congress orchestra. The only exceptions here were Henry Cowell's fresh *Hymn and Fuguing Tune* and Harry Freedman's serial, yet transparent *Tableau*.

The works written for conventional instruments, yet exploring new ways of expression, ranged from extreme abstraction to direct and warm humanity. Ernst Krenek's totally serialized piano-solo work *Sechs Vermessene* with its brittle, sporadic sound-conglomerations belongs in the first category, whereas John Weinzweig's expressive work for voice and orchestra, *Wine of Peace*, with its impassioned call to all mankind, stands at the opposite end. Between these extremes there were symmetrically reversible forms by Iain Hamilton and Jean Papineau-Couture, both lyric and tender pieces, the first in pointillistic technique, the second with intricate rhythmic patterns. There were also more percussive or glassy solutions to problems of sonority in works of Karl-Birger Blomdahl and Karl Schiske. And last, not least, two works of tremendous emotional impact and unusual constructive skill have to be mentioned: the *Duo Concertante* for violin and cello by George Rochberg and István Anhalt's *Symphony*.

It has been stated earlier in this survey that the performers chosen for these concerts executed their task in a most expert fashion with occasional flashes of greatness, a fact which was unanimously hailed by the local and international press as well as the composers present. The heaviest load was carried by the members of the National Festival Orchestra who played the first part of the opening chamber orchestra concert and who shared between themselves the assignments in the chamber music programme. A wind and percussion ensemble from Toronto rose to the occasion in preparing the intricate Varèse and Blomdahl works, and the CBC Symphony Orchestra was on hand to perform the symphonic scores.

Frederick Prausnitz from New York conducted the *Deserts* with brilliance and insight, Walter Susskind reigned authoritatively over the CBC ensemble, and Victor Feldbrill handled the chamber music fare with assurance and precision.

Of individual performers, soprano Mary Simmons from Toronto was outstanding in works by Weinzweig and Reutter, and the New York mezzo-soprano, Cathy Berberian, excelled in her superhuman role as the soloist in the electronic works by Maderna and Cage. Soprano Maria Esther Robles was the virtuoso soloist in Villa-Lobos' *Bachianas Brasilieras no. 5*.

Four Canadian instrumentalists deserve special mention in their roles as most inspired and able performers in various works: Mario Bernardi as the soloist in Jean Papineau-Couture's *Piece Concertante* for piano and strings, William Aide in Karl-Birger Blomdahl's *Chamber Concerto* for piano, wind, and percussion, and violinist Hyman Goodman and cellist Donald Whitton as the performers of Rochberg's *Duo Concertante*.

Composers who participated in the performances of their own works were Ernst Krenek, Hermann Reutter, Roy Harris, and Otar Taktakishvili.

The achievements of the Conference and its concerts are best summed up in the words of the eminent United States music critic, Alfred Frankenstein of the *San Francisco Chronicle*, who as guest reviewer for the *Toronto Daily Star* had the following comments to make:

The composers I especially liked number exactly 13. Of these, three (Varèse, Rochberg and Cage) are American; one (Hamilton) British; one (Blomdahl) Swedish; one (Schiske) Austrian; two (Maderna and Berio) Italian; one (Badings) Dutch; and four (Joachim, Anhalt, Freedman and Weinzweig) Canadian. It is not surprising that Canadians do well at a Canadian festival; what is surprising is that there was a Canadian festival to start with.

In 30 years' activity as music critic for U.S. newspapers, the only Canadian composer I had ever heard of was Healey Willan, whose choral works are often performed in the U.S. That there was a Canadian League of Composers was completely news to me when I was invited to the Stratford festival, and that these composers practise all manner of styles and media was an even more striking revelation.

That Canada has excellent performing musicians is, of course, a fact of which we in the U.S. are well aware, but only by hearsay; actually to experience the elegant work of the CBC Symphony and the Stratford Festival orchestra, of vocal soloists like Mary Simmons and conductors like Walter Susskind and Victor Feldbrill is something else again, and very rewarding.

In short, what this festival did was put Canada on the map, musically speaking, for those of us who came from the 19 foreign countries. As a result of it, I have no doubt but what Canadian orchestral and chamber music will figure more and more prominently on international programmes and Canadian music take its proper place in the international scheme of things. It is obviously past high time for such a development.

www.ingramcontent.com/pod-product-compliance
Lightning Source LLC
Chambersburg PA
CBHW051406070526
44584CB00023B/3312